Inquiry, Service, Leadership and Care

Inquiry, Service, Leadership and Care

PACIFIC LUTHERAN UNIVERSITY
1988 - 2008

PHILIP A. NORDQUIST

PACIFIC LUTHERAN UNIVERSITY PRESS
TACOMA, WASHINGTON

Contents

FOREWORD

Why would a small university in the Pacific Northwest founded by Norwegian Lutherans be the first to send students, simultaneously, to all seven continents? Why would this proudly Scandinavian college reach out to students in China, Namibia, and the Caribbean? How can a conspicuously Lutheran college (with "Lutheran" as its middle name) attract Catholics and evangelical Christians? Professor Nordquist's book tells the story, building on his prior work *Educating for Service*. PLU's history, with its triumphs and cautionary tales, is worth recounting at many levels.

To be sure, the book provides a gift to PLU. It preserves PLU's rich history for future Lutes. Nordquist skillfully highlights the colorful personalities, nagging problems, critical planning, and above all the great promise of the institution. In addition, the book's look back can help PLU look forward; we trust that lessons from the past can guide PLU in the future. As President Loren Anderson has observed: "Stories from the past should be re-told because they fuel tomorrow's dreams."

But this book represents more than a parochial institutional history. It provides important insights into how a college can retain both its religious affiliation and economic viability. Other schools have not been so successful. They have either lost one or the other. PLU's success is even more noteworthy because it resides in a region where the ranks of main line denominations are declining rapidly. More broadly, PLU's story shows how Martin Luther's ideas about faith, reason, and vocation still resonate in the modern world.

We are blessed not only in the telling of PLU's history but in the teller. With Professor Nordquist as reporter, the story unfolds with dry wit and insight. Professor Nordquist provides an insider's view without the insider's spin. For those of us who consider ourselves to be disciples of Nordquist this comes as no surprise. We experienced that every day in class.

PLU's mission is to educate students for lives of thoughtful inquiry, service, leadership, and care. The Board of Regents commissioned this book so that we can place that mission in its historical context and watch it unfold, hopeful in its promise for future generations and our world. *Soli Deo Gloria.*

Robert W. Gomulkiewicz
CHAIR, BOARD OF REGENTS
PACIFIC LUTHERAN UNIVERSITY

ACKNOWLEGEMENTS

During the past few years, when people suggested I should bring PLU's centennial history, *Educating for Service*, up to date, I was not receptive. I thought the actions and events of the past twenty years were too close to us to allow thoughtful conclusions about what they meant, and I was persuaded I had been too involved in what went on to be completely impartial. After some reflection I changed my mind. Important decisions have been made and changes have taken place at PLU that have shaped—and will continue to shape—the institution in important ways. What they are, and how they emerged, need to be understood. There were also triumphs that need to be remembered and cautionary tales that need to be told. I set to work. A reviewer of the centennial history said it was "forthright." I have tried to be "forthright" in this volume as well. The reader will have to decide if I have been successful.

Chapter one begins somewhat abruptly, without very much introductory material to provide context. *Educating for Service* is the back-story. This volume begins where that one leaves off, so I decided I did not have to summarize that book, or its last chapter, to write this one.

The writing of a university history is a community venture and I have received help at every turn. President Loren Anderson has been warmly supportive, as have those in his office, Assistant to the President Laura Polcyn and Executive Associate Vicky Winters. They answered questions, gathered information for the appendices, introduced me to the president's and regents' files, and helped with the transmission of chapters to and from editors. Director of Human Resource Services Teri Phillips gathered faculty information for the appendices and Controller Bob Riley did the same with financial information. Institutional Research Analyst Marie Wutzke provided graduation statistics and Archivist Kerstin Ringdahl was always able to provide the information I was looking for, and she and her staff assisted in the compilation of the list of regents in the appendices. That list stretches back to 1896.

Campus Pastor Dennis Sepper and Provost Patricia Killen provided invaluable information abut religious life and organizations on campus dealt with in chapter four; English professor Dennis Martin assisted with chapter five. Several faculty members and administrators provided information I needed at important turns in the story. They included: Bill Frame, Ann Kelleher, Laura Majovski, Douglas Oakman and Norris Peterson. I thank them all.

X

Four people require special thanks. University Photographer Jordan Hartman was helpful in various photographic and artistic ways, Print Publication Manager Stephen Hansen supervised the editorial activities that got the manuscript to the printer in appropriate form, and Art Director Simon Sung provided aesthetic decisions that are scattered all through the book. Finally and once again most important, Megan Benton agreed to serve as editor and untangle my prose as she did with *Educating for Service*. Her skill and taste are present on nearly every page.

The centennial history was dedicated to Helen and I said the reasons for that were myriad as all who knew me understood. Nothing has changed. In addition to everything else, she typed the manuscript for this volume. This book is dedicated to our sons, Christopher and Paul. Our lives would have been very dreary without them.

FOR
CHRISTOPHER AND PAUL

CHAPTER ONE

THE CENTENNIAL CELEBRATION AND AFTERWARD

Chapter One

THE CENTENNIAL CELEBRATION AND AFTERWARD

THE 1990-91 CENTENNIAL CELEBRATION was very successful. Planning began in May 1984 when a centennial committee was appointed by President William Rieke with business professor Thom Sepic as chair.[1] The university commissioned history professor Philip Nordquist to write a centennial history, and by the following October that task was begun. It also commissioned twenty history-related articles for the university publication *Scene*, to highlight important events and personalities in PLU's unfolding history. The university decided to print 5,000 copies of the history; that was 2,000 more than Washington State University printed for its 1990 centennial.

The committee began work in earnest the following September, deciding on a theme for the celebration and the events to be featured. Service soon became the primary focus; "Pacific Lutheran University Century II: Educating for Service" was selected as the theme. It quickly resonated with nearly all the institution's constituencies. A month-by-month schedule was soon organized as well; the university sponsored many activities, but schools, divisions, and departments also planned concerts, forums, lectures and publications. 1990-91 was a busy academic year.

The highlight may well have been the October 11 homecoming celebration which recognized one hundred alumni who exemplified "the diversity that is now PLU as we head into our second century of service." Alumni Association president James Hushagen said that the association intended "to make a statement on the occasion of the one hundredth birthday of the university about the diversity of our graduates who take seriously their responsibility to serve their families, communities, churches and humanity as a whole."[2] The list was intended to be not a selection of PLU's most notable alumni, but a representative cross-section of some of its most distinguished graduates. Excluded were those the association had previously honored, deceased alumni, and those employed by the university. Even with such constraints, it was an impressive list.[3]

A Pacific Lutheran University Athletic Hall of Fame was also launched at homecoming. The first four selections were legendary coach and athletic director Cliff Olson, pioneer of PLU women's athletics Rhoda Young, and the marvelous Marvs, Marvin Tommervik and Marvel Harshman, stars of the extraordinary football successes of the late 1930s and early 1940s. After World

War II Harshman coached collegiate basketball for forty years, including thirteen record-setting years at PLU. He retired from coaching in 1985 with 642 victories.

A remarkable forum, "The State of the World's Health," organized by 1957 alumnus William Foege, was held on 22 February 1991. Foege, a leader of the World Health Organization's campaign for the eradication of smallpox, former director of the Centers for Disease Control, and the 1991 executive director of the Carter Presidential Center of Emory University, put together a distinguished group of panelists. They included Jonas Salk, developer of the killed-virus poliomyelitis vaccine (who said he "would have come if only to hear Foege speak"), Daniel Callahan, Terrel Hill, Margretta M. Styles, Thomas Weller, and Salim Yusuf.[4] The program filled the entire day; it was learned and provocative. Salk asked "Are we being wise ancestors?" He concluded with hopes that wisdom return to our vocabularies and that more people undertake "living a purposeful life —and having a purpose in life."[5] The forum was followed the next day by a "Natural Sciences Graduates' Centennial Symposium." Forty-two individuals made presentations on a wide variety of scientific and mathematical subjects. Participants focused on issues and problems created by and potentially solved by science and technology, as well as the role of education in helping students address their moral and intellectual responsibilities.

The centennial history, *Educating for Service: Pacific Lutheran University, 1890-1990,* was published in May and was first available at the Q Club banquet on May 12. It was well received and reviewed in the *Pacific Northwest Quarterly, Oregon Historical Quarterly, Columbia,* and Tacoma's *News Tribune,* where popular Pacific Northwest historian Murray Morgan described it as "forthright." He noted that "among the charms of this fine book are its unobtrusive scholarly apparatus of footnotes and appendices, the subtle use of old photographs as chapter headings and the author's grave wit."[6] In 1991 the Concordia Historical Institute presented its Award of Commendation to the book, praising it as "an example to emulate."[7]

The centennial year sped by. The busy schedule was sometimes exhausting, but nearly all the events had been carefully chosen and were tastefully presented; all the university's constituencies were pleased by the end of the year. The centennial committee and its chair, Thom Sepic, deserved high marks.

DEMOGRAPHY

By the late 1980s enrollment became an institutional—and certainly an administrative—preoccupation, then a challenge, and finally a problem of significant proportions. President Rieke liked numbers and quantitative reasoning, and he often used numbers to address problems and to measure success. In November 1988 he discussed "drooping faculty pay" and lagging spending for the library with the *Mooring Mast*.[8] By the next April optimism about institutional growth and progress carried the day. He told the *Mast* he envisioned a student body of five thousand by the turn of the century. "Tremendous growth has been and will continue to be a large part of the Rieke administration." The growth would be "straight line" and "managed," and space and staff issues would have to be addressed. He concluded the interview with one of his favorite catch phrases. The institution is much better known, he said; unlike when he assumed the presidency, he rarely heard "PLWho?"[9] Veteran faculty members who weren't so sure the institution was veiled in obscurity in the 1960s and 1970s often bristled when they heard the phrase. Enrollment the following September seemed to support Rieke's enthusiasm; there was a 4.8 percent increase to more than four thousand students. The previous year 1021 students had received degrees, the first leap over one thousand in total graduates.[10]

The tide began to turn in 1989, however. Freshman enrollment dropped by sixty, but there was no sharp reaction. Indeed, Rieke expressed concern about campus growth and said the institution should not become too large. He urged an enrollment cap in the next five years, probably at five thousand.[11] Enrollment decline continued. In September 1990 it was down 5 percent, from 3,855 students to 3,663; the freshman class was down 20 percent, prompting a 6 percent budget cut. Large graduating classes and smaller first-year classes now began to exacerbate the situation more dramatically. "Affordability" was thought to be the main problem.[12]

Why was the situation not anticipated? The president said the answer was "simple": "it was anticipated as a possibility, but the history of ten consecutive years of enrollment growth in the face of similar warning flags, plus the genuine desire to improve salaries led to conscious choice of the present budget practices together with their risks."[13] The enrollment facts are clear, however, and we must react to them, he said.

In late September a fascinating exchange of letters between President Rieke and economics professors Norris Peterson and Donald Wentworth addressed the enrollment problem and discussed the use of more financial aid as a solution. Peterson and Wentworth laid out the argument very carefully. Rieke expressed his gratitude for their "interest in exploring . . . a tuition discount model by which to increase enrollment (and revenue), and for the very real courtesy of telling me about it in advance of the September 20 forum." He laid out three methods that could be used to address the financial situation. All had problems. He then discussed the tuition discount approach. It was already in place, he said, but should not be pushed even harder. It produced larger enrollments, but he felt increased financial aid drove down "the dollars that were available to other programmatic needs." After a series of quantitatively reasoned case studies, Rieke concluded about tuition discounting (or more use of financial aid): "Projected over time, such progressions produce a non-viable situation. . . . [In] short, but most importantly, tuition discounting provides only immediate and limited gains, and can cause very negative longer-term consequences."[14]

Peterson and Wentworth responded very quickly: "we would like to pursue your own simple model and interpret it in the light of economic analysis." Their conclusions directly opposed Rieke's.

> There is a fundamental error in concluding that dollars spent on financial aid are like dollars spent on salaries or building maintenance or supplies . . . dollars spent on financial aid can attract even more dollars . . . it is not appropriate to think of financial aid as cost when making decisions. Rather, it should be considered as smaller increases in revenue than one would get with full-pay students but with no impact on the cost side . . . Our conclusion is simple. The university could, if it chose to do so, bring more students and more revenue to the university with no real cost.[15]

More letters followed, with discussions about the use and meaning of language and how much their positions agreed, but Rieke was still concerned about the long-term negative results of too much discounting and that financial aid might take away from "program." "We do in fact agree more than we disagree," Peterson clarified, "but we do continue to disagree most strongly with one point you make."[16] That point was Rieke's understanding of program dollars. There is no evidence the Peterson-Wentworth advice was taken, and enrollment continued to be a problem.

In October Rieke ordered a hiring freeze until a long-term solution to the budget problems could be found. A $1.5 million cut for the 1991-92 budget was announced, along with a 15 percent cut in staff and administrative payroll, but the president insisted it was not "financial doomsday."[17] He met with faculty to squelch rumors and provide information. There was a concerned and outspoken response. Physics and mathematics professor Chang-Li Yiu said PLU was "drifting" and its growth was "aimless"; focus was on the quantity of programs, not their quality.[18]

By the next September in his state of the university address Rieke said the worst of the crisis was over. The university was back in the black: "not only was financial disaster avoided, but the university actually became stronger."[19] The president's optimism was encouraging, but it reflected a short-term fix. Enrollment and budgets would require serious attention for at least the next decade.

Peterson and Wentworth continued to address enrollment strategies; they met new President Loren Anderson in March 1993 to discuss strategies, then urged him "to use what accountants call 'unfunded financial aid' to improve enrollment at PLU. The risk and cost are quite low while the benefits are potentially very high."[20] Anderson thanked them for their commitment and creative contributions to the complicated issue.

THE HUNTHAUSEN CONTROVERSY

On 5 April 1990, Robert Stivers, acting for the religion department, submitted the name of Raymond G. Hunthausen, Roman Catholic archbishop of Seattle, for an honorary doctorate. He was an appealing, but for some a controversial, candidate. The faculty unanimously supported the nomination, and it was sent on to the board of regents for its imprimatur.

Hunthausen was born in Montana; he graduated from Carroll College in Helena in 1943 and was ordained in 1946. He served as coach, athletic director, professor of chemistry, and, from 1957-1962, president of Carroll College. He attended the Second Vatican Council as the sixth bishop of Helena and was appointed archbishop of Seattle in 1975. His admirers thought of him as "the quintessential Vatican II bishop."[21]

During his fifteen years of administration in Seattle there was intense activity, including shared decision-making among clergy and laity regarding pro-life concerns, ecumenism, evangelization through the mass media, housing for the poor and elderly, women's roles, ministry to and advocacy of the rights of racial and sexual minorities, the nuclear arms race, southeast Asian refugees, and sanctuary. Most dramatic, or at least most controversial, was Hunthausen's involvement in the peace movement and his withholding of 50 percent of his personal federal income tax in protest of United States involvement in the nuclear arms race. His leadership excited and encouraged many, but not all. Numerous complaints were sent to Rome by a variety of both clergy and lay people.

Correspondence between Seattle and the Vatican about pastoral practice and the presentation of church teaching began in 1978. A number of areas of concern emerged: the activity of the Tribunal, liturgy, clergy formation, priests leaving the ministry, moral issues in health care institutions, and ministry to homosexuals. The issues were doctrinal and pastoral; nuclear weapons and taxation were not included in the ultimate apostolic visitation that took place. The result of that visitation was the transfer of authority in the five areas of concern to an auxiliary bishop "to promote the building up of the church in Seattle in harmony with the universal church." Withholding of taxes and civil disobedience became the key issues for PLU regents, not pastoral practices or doctrine.

At their April 15 meeting, after a long debate, the regents voted 19 to 6 not to award the doctorate. It was the board's only honorary degree denial in the institution's history. At the same meeting the board approved awarding honorary degrees to Queen Sonja of Norway and Gunnar Stallsett, the general secretary of the Lutheran World Federation.

Reaction to the board's action was almost instantaneous. The major Pacific Northwest newspapers featured the story. Tacoma's *News Tribune* said the refusal was related to "his outspoken views on U.S. military spending and his sometimes stormy relationship with the Vatican." Other papers agreed. Lutheran clergy in the area were outraged. A petition signed by twenty-one pastors and lay people protested the board's decision because of Hunthausen's "acts of civil disobedience in protest of military spending." The petition urged the board to reconsider its decision. Sharply worded letters came from ten influential Lutheran pastors: "the Board struck out," "a missed opportunity," "I read with disgust," "deep disappointment." Harvey Neufeld, vice president for church relations, wrote to Rieke that "some form of damage control needs to be considered." The faculty petitioned the board for an explanation and dialogue. Neither was forthcoming. In university life, where both are staples, that was unfortunate.

There were only two public responses by the board. In a letter to Jeffrey Smith, widely known as the Frugal Gourmet, who was "hurt and dismayed" by the refusal, board chair David Wold wrote:

> I regret the hurt and dismay that the decision of the P.L.U. regents has brought to you. Your concern is shared by a number of persons who have corresponded with us. The action . . . came after long and vigorous discussion. The members of the Board expressed their consciences just as did the members of the faculty. In this instance those consciences expressed themselves quite differently from each other . . . what shall we do when consciences collide?[22]

In an interview with the *Mooring Mast* Wold said the board used a combination of data, persuasive logic, and feelings to reach the decision.[23] The only support for board action came from a dozen letters, from Roman Catholics who were dismayed by Hunthausen's attempted reform activities and civil disobedience.

One change came out of the acrimonious atmosphere of April and May. Faculty legislation governing the awarding of honorary degrees was rewritten to include more board-faculty discussion and exchange of information before final votes were taken. The new language and procedures have served the institution well. The board did not reconsider or further explain its action.

ACADEMIC AND CAMPUS LIFE

In 1988 the university launched a nationwide search to replace retiring provost Richard Jungkuntz after nineteen years of service. It was hoped this and three 1987 vice presidential appointments (finance and operations, student life, and church relations) would help maintain institutional momentum and carry PLU past the centennial celebration into the last decade of the twentieth century. Of more than one hundred provost nominations, ninety-nine were considered (seven were women), and four were brought to campus: John Yost, vice chancellor for research and dean of the graduate school at the University of Nebraska; Francis Tuggle, dean of the Jones Graduate School of Administration at Rice University; Kathleen Dubs, vice president for academic affairs and dean of the faculty at Cedar Crest College; and J. Robert Wills, dean of the College of Fine Arts at the University of Texas at Austin. The search committee, headed by economics professor Ernest Ankrim, recommended Wills, who accepted the appointment, effective 15 July 1989.

Wills was a 1962 graduate of the College of Wooster with a Ph.D. degree from Case-Western Reserve University in dramatic art. He had taught, published widely, directed or produced more than four hundred plays, and served in various administrative positions at Wittenberg University, the University of Kentucky, and the University of Texas. In a wide-ranging telephone interview with *Mooring Mast* editor Matt Misterek, Wills responded to a mission statement question:

> I think there must be a way for PLU to glory in its Lutheran heritage while celebrating its Christian character, and at the same time protect the rights—indeed I would go further than that and say champion the rights—of those with different beliefs, alternative ideas, and equally strong, if contrasting, convictions.[24]

He set to work in July.

In April it was announced that 1985 graduate Elizabeth Pulliam had received a Pulitzer Prize, along with several colleagues from the *Anchorage Daily News*. They had written a ten-part series (which took six months to put together) about alcoholism and suicide among Alaskan natives. Pulliam said she went to Alaska because she needed "adventure" and then "fell in love with the place." Alaskans respect fighters and aggressive people, she said. The reporters had to fight with the editor to get the story approved. Pulliam expressed gratitude to journalism professor Cliff Rowe; "He trained us so well as reporters that the transition from school to the job didn't feel so different."[25] Gratitude toward Rowe is shared by a remarkable number of journalism graduates.

In November of 1989 the footprint of PLU in Parkland became larger with the purchase of the Parkland Elementary School for $1.7 million. $375 thousand of the cost was met by the transfer in lieu of cash of approximately 5.5 acres of PLU land contiguous to the Keithley Junior High School buildings and west of the PLU golf course. The elementary school soon came to be called the East Campus, and it became a center of multiple activities on the edge of busy Pacific Avenue.

In January of 1990 PLU received the largest single gift in the institution's history up to that time ($1.8 million). It came from Mary Baker Russell and her brother Elbert H. Baker II; the Bakers and Russells had been deeply involved in the operation of the Tacoma's *News Tribune* over many decades. The gift kicked off the public phase of the $30 million "Shaping Tomorrow" centennial campaign. A $5.5 million badly needed music building, a centerpiece of the campaign, would be named the Mary Baker Russell Music Center.[26] It would take until the mid-1990s to complete the fund raising and building, but the enterprise was launched. A new music building, which music department chair David Robbins had been promised as a prospective faculty member in 1969, would now become reality.

The late 1980s brought challenges and changes to the campus and dramatic changes to the larger world. In November 1989 the Berlin Wall came down and 1989 graduate and Fulbright Scholar Christian Lucky saw it fall. Interviewed by Seattle radio and television stations, he said the attitude was "euphoric"; he walked on the wall (an "incredible feeling") and predicted that economic differences in the two parts of Germany would become a major issue.[27]

International studies, which had been growing rapidly since the late 1970s, made another leap forward at this time. Fourteen PLU students were accepted for study in the recently announced Baltic Program as Samantha Smith Scholars. Samantha Smith was a New England girl who charmed the world with her plea for peace sent to Soviet leader Yuri Andropov; when she visited the Soviet Union and was later killed in a plane crash, the program was named in her honor. Political science professor Donald Farmer was selected to be the program's director in residence in Riga, Latvia (Farmer was soon studying Latvian to add to the long list of languages he knew); political science professor Ann Kelleher visited Lithuania in April, and business professor Eli Berniker traveled to Estonia. The exchange was funded by the U.S. Information Agency.[28] The next year eleven Baltic students studied at PLU for a semester in a program designed by business school dean Gundar King (a Latvian who fled the country in 1944 ahead of advancing Soviet armies). Eight studied business and three computer science. By September 1990 four PLU students were back from studying in Lithuania. They had experienced the break with the Soviet Union; they described a "subdued reaction" and said people were waiting to see what was going to happen next.

Concern about the possibility of war in the Middle East—what came to be called "Operation Desert Storm"—also began to trouble the nation and the campus. On 15 January 1991 President Rieke wrote a deeply moving memorandum to the PLU community:

> In the desperate but now almost certainly vain hope that something will avert war in the Persian Gulf, I address faculty, staff and students . . . on the somber and frightful topic of PLU and war . . . What shall the community and institu-

tion of Pacific Lutheran University do . . . The first is to continue what you are doing . . . the second is to recognize that it is important to discuss openly and freely our differing view points, and to express our support or opposition in reasoned, respectful and useful settings . . . third, let us, as never previously, support one another and pray for peace.[29]

The war came and the Middle East continues to be fractured by war, terrorism, and violence.

In February 1991 violence hit Parkland. Six students were shot while attending a party near the campus. After being told he was not welcome at the party, a twenty-year-old Spanaway man sprayed the crowd with a .22 caliber semi-automatic rifle. The police described the event as a "random shooting." Twelve cars were also vandalized. None of the students was seriously injured.

February was also the cultural high point of the year with the performance of music professor Greg Youtz's opera, "Songs From the Cedar House." Based on Northwest Indian culture and environment, it began with a creation story derived from legends and concluded in present-day Seattle. Traditional costumes and settings were combined with the use of lasers. Youtz had worked on the project for several years.

Athletics continued to flourish in the late 1980s, especially women's athletics. In 1988 the women's fast-pitch softball team won the National Association of Intercollegiate Athletics (NAIA) national title with a 2-0 victory over Minnesota-Duluth. Coach Ralph Weekly's Lady Lutes were 5-0 in the winners' bracket with a 39-6 season record. Senior catcher Karen Stout was the tournament MVP and PLU's first softball all-American; Weekly was named coach of the year. This softball success would continue—between 1987 and 2003 the Lady Lutes won sixteen Northwest Conference championships.

The women's soccer successes were even more dramatic. Coach Colleen Hacker, who came to PLU in 1979 to teach physical education and coach field hockey, had to learn soccer on the fly after field hockey was dropped from the program and soccer was added. Learn she did. Soccer was just beginning to boom in the nation and the Northwest. Between 1981 and 1992 the women's team won ten conference championships and three national (NAIA) championships (1988, 1989, and 1991). They were runners-up twice (1990 and 1992). Hacker was national coach of the year in 1989. Those teams featured a cluster of outstanding players, but especially noteworthy were Sonya Brandt, a four-time all-American who still holds all of the PLU scoring records; Wendy Johnson, a two-time all-American, third in career scoring; and Cheryl Kragness, a 1992 all-American, fourth in career scoring and an academic all-American. The teams featured numerous academic all-Americans.

Also in 1988 PLU women won the NAIA award for the top athletic program among members, based on the school's success in ten varsity sports. On the strength of five men's and five women's championships, PLU athletes had already won the Northwest Conference's All Sports award for the third straight year.

The football teams with coach Frosty Westering in charge continued to compete at the highest level. The 1987 team won a national championship, the 1991 team was a runner-up, and the 1993 team won another national championship in an over-whelming fashion. On the way to the title the team defeated Cumberland 61-7, Central Washington 35-17 and Baker 52-14. The title game was played in Memorial Coliseum in Portland, Oregon, where PLU defeated Westminister College of Pennsylvania 50-20. Marc Weekly was the offensive star of that team; a four-year starter at quarterback, he holds nearly all of the offensive and passing records for the Lutes. He was a 1993 all-American. There were 26 all-Americans during Westering's coaching years.

Questions about the identity of PLU and the meaning of its Lutheran heritage continued to be raised, especially by the *Mooring Mast,* as part of a long editorial tradition. In the next several years it would become an issue involving most of PLU's constituencies. In November 1990 the *Mast* included a supplement entitled "What's Lutheran About PLU?" It included several extensive and thoughtful articles, graphs, and comparisons with Seattle Pacific University and the University of Puget Sound.[30] President Rieke also addressed the topic:

> Lutheran Christians believe that the foundation of their personal existence—the warp and the woof of life, if you like—is to be found in the correct understanding of the word vocation . . . Vocation is "to call" and vocation is calling. And so by our faith each of us is called . . . called by my baptism to serve God.[31]

THE FRoG COMMITTEE

By the late 1980s colleges and universities around the country became increasingly concerned about the nature of their calendars and curricula. What was so intellectually and morally important that all students needed to know it? What should be in the core curriculum? Institutions like Columbia University, the University of Chicago, and Stanford University were among the leaders in this enterprise, and they examined their core programs in an exceedingly critical fashion. Their contemporary and Western Civilization programs stretched back to the educational reforms that emerged after World War I. Those programs and others like them had been very influential for many years. Would they now be changed in the face of multiple pressures? PLU, which addresses these issues in a relatively cyclical fashion, decided it was time to rethink its core curriculum. How should it be packaged? Should new emphases be included?

That task had last been attempted in the midst of the ferment and reform of the 1960s. Then it was approached with considerable optimism; the entire curriculum—certainly the core curriculum—had not changed appreciably since the mid-1930s, and students and most faculty seemed to favor changes. After the 1965 Faculty Fall Conference discussed the need for change, in September President Robert Mortvedt appointed a ten-person committee, chaired by history professor Walter Schnackenberg, to produce a new core. The committee reported in spring 1966 with a radical restructuring that included non-curricular activities and vacations in its scheme. It encouraged interdisciplinary seminars and independent research, and it minimized the importance of grades in lower-division courses. The committee stressed that the proposal was very broad and ideal and that much of the substance would have to be worked out by the faculty. There would be a junior-level written examination covering six areas of study. Campus social and dormitory life was included in the scheme. The proposal was called SCOPEXAM VI.[32]

Many members of the faculty were chary. The proposal was received but not approved by a faculty vote. Its critics said it was "unrealistic" and "unworkable"; its supporters said it would permit thoughtfulness and creativity. New committees were appointed and the reform process dragged on until 1969. The previous year a 4-1-4 calendar was adopted as was a course system. A new core was finally adopted on 23 April 1969. It featured a seven-course distribution requirement, not substantially different from the old system: science, literature, history, religion, philosophy, and English composition.

> The dreams and hopes of translating the statement of objectives into curricular and campus reality had been dashed by a variety of practical and intellectual disagreements and ongoing disagreements between the College of Arts and Sciences and the professional schools. The new curriculum, while serviceable, was a political compromise.[33]

That core, slightly modified, was still in place in 1989 when the faculty decided reform was needed. A somewhat clumsy nineteen-member committee—The Faculty Committee for Restructuring of the General University Requirements—was appointed in February 1989, with the president and provost as advisory members. The title was soon shortened to the FRoG Committee, in part because of committee chair Robert Stivers's enthusiasm for frogs.

The committee set to work immediately. There were presentations at the Faculty Fall Conference, hearings, meetings, and individual conversations. Sixteen organizing principles were established; it was announced that four skills would be emphasized and eleven understandings nurtured by the general university requirements. Two core models were presented to the faculty in November 1990.

The faculty should choose one model for further development, the committee said, before final action in the spring.

The spring proposal included eight areas of study: reasoning and writing, science and the scientific method, the western heritage, cross-cultural perspectives, human diversity, ethics and philosophy, self-expression, physical education, and a capstone course. It would total 46 to 48 credits. Some old core courses and sequences were eliminated and some new arrangements were added. There was a strong reaction, both positive and negative. The Integrated Studies Program and the 4-1-4 calendar would be retained.

April 1991 was filled with memoranda, meetings, and parliamentary procedure. Memos from the sciences criticized the reduction of the laboratory science requirement to one course; the religion department and others expressed concerns about adequate depth in religion with only one required course; and memos, petitions, and proposed amendments lamented the absence of literature as an "important way of knowing," as one English professor phrased it.[34]

The April 26 faculty meeting was lively. After much speaking and numerous amendments about the writing seminar, diversity requirements, and science and the scientific method, the meeting was postponed at 6:00 pm until 3 May. At that meeting the proposal was referred back to the committee.

The FroG Committee revised the proposal considerably and included it in the February 1992 faculty meeting agenda. Also included was an alternative proposal drafted by philosophy professor Paul Menzel and English professor Paul Benton; it was closer to the old core. Again much discussion and further delays ensued. In April the FroG proposal was defeated 73-53 and the Benton-Menzel alternative was accepted. It included the comprehensive first year experience segment from the FroG proposal and new cross cultural and alternative perspectives requirements. Stivers said, with some disappointment, "the faculty elected to pursue a more traditionally oriented, less ambitious path."[35] It would be fifteen years before the faculty took up the core curriculum again.

RESIGNATION

In May 1990, with the centennial celebrations about to begin, but with enrollment and budgets posing serious problems, President William Rieke signed on for three more years. He said his most difficult decisions as president were about people, followed by tuition hikes and the budget. He was optimistic about the future; he spoke about the emergence of an engineering program, a music building, a new dormitory, and an envisioned worship center. In the midst of enrollment problems he expressed concern about campus growth; the institution should not become too large. Enrollment would have to be capped in the next five years, perhaps at five thousand.[36]

In November the president called for the creation of a Presidential Strategic Advisory Commission to advise him on budgetary matters and the future direction of the university, and to draft a new university statement of objectives. The current statement was thirty years old and dated. The commission would have ten members: six faculty, two staff, one administrator, and one student. The members would serve for two years. "The PSAC will be an organization of major significance in the history of the university, and will receive direct and continued support and contact from myself."[37] The commission was operating by April; budget advice was intermittent and soon faded away. Crafting a new statement of objectives would consume much time and energy over the next two years; it would land in the lap of a new president in 1992.[38]

In the midst of all that was happening President Rieke continued to be optimistic: "I assure you that we will continue to be a strong, stable and solvent university financially, and that the excellent academic reputation built by our highly qualified faculty will be sustained. Building on the realistic base of 3,400 students for 1991-92, and 3,200 students thereafter, the institution will remain entirely consistent with its mission."[39]

On 15 April at the spring meeting of the board of regents President Rieke announced his retirement, effective 30 June 1992. He decided to retire because of changes the university was undergoing: "The '90s are going to bring many changes. The leadership of the university should be around to plan and implement, as well as live with those changes." The financial situation did not "push me to do it," he told the *Mooring Mast*.[40] Many faculty and staff wondered if it wasn't lurking in the background, however. Also in April the *Mast* received numerous letters about the budget. The letters were especially critical of the finance and operations office and leadership.[41]

A presidential search committee was created in May and worked industriously over the summer; it was hoped the selection of a new president could be accomplished by December. The president made two suggestions about what was going on in his September 1991 "state of the university" address: first, he hoped the president's role in faculty deliberations would not be diminished (he was especially concerned about not changing the president's chairing of monthly faculty meetings); second, on a more personal note, he hoped the university would "extend the new president the same quality and extent of courtesy and support I enjoyed from this community during my transition and learning years."[42]

William O. Rieke returned to his *alma mater* as president in 1975 because he thought he could help create for others the undergraduate experience he had received. He came in the midst of turbulent times, both at PLU and nationally.[43] He helped bring order and calm to the campus and confidence to the university's various constituencies; he was very important in encouraging the growth, experimentation, and expansion that marked the late 70s and 80s. His credentials as a major medical researcher and administrator brought prestige and confidence to the institution at a difficult but important time in its history.

The achievements that emerged during his seventeen-year presidency are impressive. They included accreditation for the School of Business's MBA and accounting programs, a growing international emphasis, and purchase of East Campus. During his presidency the $8.9 million William O. Rieke Science Center was completed, Ramstad Hall was remodeled, the Scandinavian Cultural Center was created in the basement of the University Center, a third floor was added to the library, the Names Fitness Center was built, KPLU went from forty thousand to one hundred thousand watts, and groundbreaking took place for the Mary Baker Russell Music Center.

Rieke said that on 30 June 1992 he would hand over the keys and get on with retirement. He had been free to make his own mistakes and he intended to extend the same freedom to his successor. In May he announced he had accepted a part-time job as director of the Cheney Foundation. He served in that position for ten years. In his final interview with the *Mooring Mast* he said there were some personnel decisions that he would change if he could, but he would not have done differently in any of the "big directions."[44]

Reactions from the faculty and staff varied. Not all were confident about recent budgetary and enrollment decisions, and many felt that both he and the institution had not received sound vice presidential financial advice, but all knew the institution had grown, spread its wings, and gained in confidence during his presidency. The faculty and staff wished him well in retirement.[45] The board of regents did the same, thanking the president for his years of service, naming him president emeritus, and presenting him with a Ford Ranger XL truck. It also honored Lucille Giroux for her thirty two years of service to the university and five of its presidents, starting with Seth Eastvold. She was named executive associate emeritus. Retiring development vice president Luther Bekemeier was named vice president emeritus.[46]

CHAPTER TWO

A New President, Old Problems,
Interesting Beginnings

Chapter Two

A New President, Old Problems,
Interesting Beginnings

Following the April 1991 announcement by President William Rieke that he would retire on 30 June 1992, the board of regents authorized board chair David Wold to select a committee to search for PLU's twelfth president. The selection process went smoothly and was completed by 30 May. The faculty elected two representatives: Philip Nordquist, professor of history, and Sheri Tonn, professor of chemistry. The other members were appointed by Wold. They included board members Dr. Cynthia Edwards, a Tacoma physician; Frank Jennings (the committee chair), an Eddie Bauer executive; and Gary Severson, a banking executive. (Jennings, Severson, and Edwards would all be future board chairs.) James Hushagen, a Tacoma attorney, was the alumni representative; Patricia Roundy, director of the Aura program at PLU, was the staff representative; Pastor Martin Wells represented the campus ministry; and Scott Friedman, the ASPLU president, represented the students. Wold was an ex officio member. The committee set to work immediately. Jennings was an effective and energetic chair, and Friedman represented student perspectives with vigor and wit; he more than held his own in the enterprise.

One of the first decisions was to hire a search firm to help organize the selection process and identify candidates. After hearing presentations from several firms the committee selected the Academic Search Consultation Service of Washington, D.C.; the ASCS staff went to work quickly. They read reams of material, visited campus, and interviewed President Rieke, the vice presidents, a number of regents, pastors, department chairs, the development staff, alumni, and students. This activity produced a 5 August 1991 confidential report that summarized the current situation at PLU and laid out a search and selection process. The search committee found the report very helpful.

The ASCS report asserted that "PLU is a very different place than it was when President Rieke was inaugurated—larger, stronger, and better known in the region and across the country." It was fortunate, the report noted, that the search would be conducted against the backdrop of a highly successful long-term presidency. It advised the committee to take a long-range view; the short-term experience of enrollment downturn and concentration on economies should not deflect the search's focus on what PLU would become in the twenty-first century.

Fundraising and planning priorities had quickly emerged from the interviews and discussions, but the ASCS stressed that both numbers and dollars should be seen as results not purposes of the university. It also urged a clearer focus of academic programs and a more deliberate role for development, which should not simply be the by-product of aggressive entrepreneurship in a setting of rapid enrollment growth.

The report concluded with eleven presidential qualities, characteristics, or skills that should guide the search. Planning, fundraising, and enrollment management came first, then strengthening and focusing of academic programs, followed by administrative, fiscal, and communication skills. It strongly emphasized that the relationship with the Evangelical Lutheran Church in America (ELCA) should be sustained.[1] The search committee took the report and these emphases very seriously in its deliberations and decisions.

The search was launched in the summer with two advertisements in the *Chronicle of Higher Education* and four hundred letters sent to leaders in higher education requesting names of possible candidates. By the middle of October ninety-seven nominations had been received; screening and reference checking had reduced the list to twenty names. Further analysis reduced the number to eight candidates, who were brought to Tacoma on 21 and 27 October for off-campus interviews. These took place in Frank Jennings's basement family room in a tightly organized fashion with each committee member responsible for one line of questioning (planning, fundraising, enrollment management, and so on). The intense sessions were exhausting to the committee, and undoubtedly to the candidates, but the process worked well and unanimity was reached on the three candidates to bring to campus: Ryan C. Amacher, Loren J. Anderson, and Kenneth W. Tolo. The committee thought it was an outstanding trio.

Ryan Amacher was dean of the College of Commerce and Industry and professor of economics at Clemson University. Earlier he had been at the University of Arizona and the University of Oklahoma. A graduate of Ripon College, his Ph.D. degree was from the University of Virginia. He had been an economist for the U.S. Treasury and had held international lectureships in Romania, China, Barbados, France, Colombia, and Guatemala. He had served on commissions related to economic development in South Carolina, Arizona, and Alaska, and he had written extensively—several economics textbooks (one competed with PLU economics professor Stanley Brue's best-selling text) and a host of articles related to higher education, the labor market, public policy issues, and international affairs.

Loren Anderson was a native of Rugby, North Dakota. He received his B.A. degree from Concordia College in philosophy, his M.A. degree from Michigan State University in rhetoric and public address, and his Ph.D. degree from the University of Michigan in communication theory and research. He taught at

Wayne State University for one year, then returned to Concordia to serve in a variety of capacities: director of institutional research, assistant to the president, and
vice president for planning and development. (At thirty-one he was the youngest
vice president in Concordia history.) From 1984 to 1988 he served the American Lutheran Church, first as executive director of college and university services, then as national director of the "Commitment to Mission" fund drive. He
returned to Concordia in 1988 as executive vice president with responsibilities
for fund development, communication, academic planning, and general administration. In both periods of service at Concordia he was heavily involved
with its widely imitated "Blueprint" planning process and its program of affir-
mative action. He was the co-author of a communication textbook and author
of a number of articles about communication and higher education.

Kenneth Tolo was also a B.A. graduate of Concordia College, but in mathematics; his M.A. and Ph.D. degrees, also in mathematics, were from the University of Nebraska. He received an M.A. degree in public affairs from the
University of Minnesota and a management certificate from Harvard, and he
completed the executive program of the graduate school of business at Stanford
and the Japanese language program at Dartmouth. In 1972 he began teaching
in the Lyndon B. Johnson School of Public Affairs at the University of Texas at
Austin. There he also served in a variety of administrative positions: associate
vice president for academic affairs, associate vice president for academic affairs
and research, and vice provost. He had worked for the German Marshall Fund
and the U.S. Department of Commerce. Tolo was the son and grandson of
Lutheran pastors.[2]

The candidates were brought to campus in the middle of November; each
had a tightly organized two-day series of meetings. They met with President
Rieke, the vice presidents, the provost, various faculty groups, pastors, alumni,
students, and the search committee. Dozens of faculty, staff, and students responded. Some comments were brief and impressionistic, but most were carefully thought through. Interestingly, support was equally divided among the
three candidates.

Kenneth Tolo's planning, budgetary, and management skills were obvious, as
was his ability to work collegially with others. It was clear that he would attempt
to maintain a close connection to the Lutheran church. Those who thought the
new president should help bring sharper focus and greater discipline to academic
life favored his candidacy. Loren Anderson emphasized moving beyond the goal of
growth that had dominated the recent past and maintaining and building on the
institution's Lutheran tradition. His planning and fundraising experience and his
service at an institution like PLU resonated with many, especially students, alumni,
and regents. Ryan Amacher, confident and often outspoken, seemed like a fresh
breeze to those who thought that significant change was necessary at this stage of

PLU's history. The range of his experience was broad and appealing.

The *Mast* reported on student sessions carefully and perceptively. Tolo was described as "soft spoken and unassuming" and optimistic about solving budget difficulties. He thought the church relationship should be fostered. Students were impressed with how extensively he had done his homework and, according to ASPLU vice president Burley Kawasaki, how sharp he was. Some were concerned about his approachability. Sophomore Monica Ricarte considered him a little intimidating. Anderson was described as "amiable." He characterized PLU as one of the "flagships" of Lutheran higher education and stressed planning, moving beyond growth emphases, and working with his wife, MaryAnn, as a team. Students liked his understanding of the PLU community and his goal setting and fundraising abilities. Ricarte thought Anderson would be more receptive to the student viewpoint than the other candidates. Amacher said a president should be off-campus raising money, and he considered the five-year plan "a wish list." He was vague about PLU's Lutheran ties; as Ricarte perceived it, "He didn't want to start a religious revival, but wanted to know the business side of things. If Amacher was president, we would turn into another UPS." Senior James Toycen said, "He would be really good for a public institution, but he's not a PLU type of guy."[3] Amacher produced strong reactions both positive and negative.

After the campus visits the search committee developed more questions for the candidates and conducted more phone conversations with colleagues. The ASCS staff assisted with this follow-up activity, as did the ELCA's division for education. Committee chair Frank Jennings thought the interviews had gone well, but he felt that the campus community should have been better prepared for the visits by being asked to "base their judgments on the eleven desired characteristics." That failure produced a range of responses.[4]

After two long and carefully argued sessions in mid-December the search committee unanimously recommended to the board of regents that Loren Anderson should be PLU's next president, and on 16 December Tacoma's *News Tribune* announced: "Fund-raiser, planner selected to become new PLU president." In a telephone interview Anderson told the paper he was "looking forward to fine-tuning PLU programs and building stronger financial moorings. . . . The basic strengths are all there . . . I am really bullish about the place." Board chair David Wold said he was delighted with the selection and that Anderson most clearly fit the criteria formulated for the position.[5]

Anderson visited campus in January 1992 and met with the board, outlining a three-point plan for the next several months. He would: (1) answer phone calls and letters and put his snow blower and house up for sale, (2) attempt to meet as many members of the PLU family as possible, and (3) study PLU's history.[6]

The inauguration of Loren Anderson as the twelfth president of Pacific

Lutheran University took place on 8 September 1992. Opening convocation and the inauguration ceremony were merged in a dramatic fashion. The ceremony began, with emeritus music professor Larry Meyer's "Procession of Joy." There were greetings, anthems, and Concordia College's videotaped "Introduction of Loren J. Anderson to Pacific Lutheran University." The Rev. Dr. Herbert Chilstrom, presiding bishop of the Evangelical Lutheran Church in America, performed the rite of inauguration and board chair David Wold and Provost J. Robert Wills presented the presidential seal. Symbolic gifts to the university followed. They came from the church (all six bishops of Region I of the ELCA were present), Governor Booth Gardner, County Executive Joe Stortini, State Superintendent of Schools Judith Billings (a PLU alumna), students, faculty, and alumni. Faculty representative history professor Christopher Browning presented a copy of the eloquent and prophetic statement about the necessary dialectical relationship of faculty and presidents that Walter Schnackenberg had read at Eugene Wiegman's inauguration in 1970. It captured the attention of all, though some thought it inappropriate on a celebratory day. Browning read:

> If you go too fast, we shall slow things down.
> If you go too slowly, we shall speed things up.
> If you want answers, we shall give you more questions.
> If you want a motion, we shall give you an amendment.
> If you become high-handed, we shall remind you of our ancient prerogatives.
> If you want a revolution, we shall magnify the tradition.
> If you will not change, we shall lead the revolt.[7]

Anderson's inaugural address was entitled "PLU's Viable Saga." After a careful summary of the institution's history and its founder's vision, he said: "PLU's 102 years embody this university's viable saga—a story of faith and high purpose, a story of determination in the face of challenge, a story of both personal and corporate delays and disappointments, and amidst it all, a legacy of remarkable achievements."[8]

The stories from the past should be retold, he said, because they fuel tomorrow's dreams: "We are called to be the visionaries and dreamers, the saga writers of this time and in the days that lie ahead."[9] In conclusion he sketched his hopes and dreams for the university, including academic excellence, quality throughout the university, successful fusing of liberal and professional education, continuation of the church-relatedness, the centrality of vocation to the institution's educational vision, and that the faith-reason dialectic should fuel identity. These emphases quickly became an outline for Anderson's descriptions of PLU and decision making.

Greetings at a luncheon following the convocation and inauguration ceremony included one from President Emeritus Rieke. Visibly angry about the themes in the Schnackenberg statement, he gave a forceful counter-recommendation to the new president, telling him to be the "decider;" faculty should not decide important matters.[10]

Search committee chair Frank Jennings was delighted with the inauguration. As he wrote to the committee:

> I beamed from ear to ear as I received congratulations, on your behalf, from many persons from the campus community, who enthusiastically claimed that we "found just the right person" . . . thank you again for your tremendous contribution to this extremely important process, and its very happy and fruitful conclusion. I will be forever grateful for the experience, and the partnership and friendship that I have enjoyed with each of you.[11]

The committee members agreed that their service had been both successful and unusually positive. The *Mast* was also upbeat. Editor Kim Bradford wrote that PLU stood poised for a change: "the years ahead won't be easy, but won't be dull either. The party may be over . . . but the excitement has just begun."[12]

In October board chair Rev. Dr. David Wold stepped down and was replaced by Frank Jennings. Wold had served on the board for two decades, eleven years as chair. President Emeritus William Rieke said, "I've known many board chairs in my various professional dealings through the years. I have never known one the equivalent of David Wold." In December at mid-year commencement exercises, Wold received the PLU Distinguished Service Award to recognize those years of service.[13]

THE MISSION STATEMENT

In November 1990 President Rieke had spelled out the tasks he wanted the newly appointed Presidential Strategic Advisory Commission to undertake. They included advising on budgetary matters, explaining the feasibility of restructuring the university, and rewriting the 1963 Statement of Objectives. Five faculty members on the commission chose to work on the objectives: Colleen Hacker, Paul Menzel, Philip Nordquist, Leon Reisberg, and Sheri Tonn.

Their work was under way by early spring. At a meeting in April Rieke noted that the Statement of Objectives was "the only official document to have had formal approval by faculty, administration and regents, and that such a statement is vital to the university for planning and accreditation purposes, as well as representing the university's contract service to students."[14] He thought a new statement would best serve the university in its second century of existence. The commission agreed. The 1963 statement had served the institution well as it moved into university status and in the struggles with President Seth Eastvold, but after thirty years it was dated.

In early June the committee spelled out the themes they thought should be present in the new statement. They included Luther's dialectical theology, educating for service and citizenship, academic freedom, Christian humanism, the relationship of a church-related institution to pluralism and secularism, the centrality of teaching, the importance of scholarship, and the need to integrate the spiritual, physical, and intellectual in education.[15] Those themes would be much worked over in the next two years.

In the spring and early summer advice poured in from faculty and staff. A first draft was distributed at the September 1991 faculty fall conference. President Rieke wanted the board of regents included in the discussion as soon as possible, and procedures to accomplish that were soon established. Commission members thought a final draft could be ready by December.[16] That turned out to be overly optimistic.[17]

Dozens of responses to the first draft soon emerged; they were exceedingly varied. Some enthusiastically embraced the statement while others rejected it as completely unacceptable. Some forceful missives implied that PLU should be a church with a formulaic definition that all should subscribe to while others wanted little or no religion. Some responses appeared to be legal briefs. Many offered advice about style and urged including language that soared.

The coupling of faith and reason produced the most intense response. Of all the paired themes in the draft, the commission members thought it the most important and had labored over it the longest, struggling to describe that relationship authentically in the early 1990s after thirty years of revolutionary change in higher education and the secularity and pluralism it accompanied.

The commission decided at its 8 October meeting to extend its timetable and schedule more conversations. Forums were set for 15 November and 6 December. The 15 November forum featured eight five-minute presentations, small group discussions, and reports back to a reconvened plenary session. The five-minute presentations were quite diverse. The 6 December forum, "Educating for Excellence—Century II," was well attended and positive in tone.

After much discussion a second draft of the mission statement was ready by mid-April 1992 and a third campus-wide forum was held on 7 May. The commission members thought the faith-reason dialectic was more understandable and the professional schools were incorporated into the statement more effectively. Paul Menzel reported to the *Mast* that the committee "did two things. First, the religious connection is more vividly stated. . . . Second, we stated it in a way that wouldn't make others feel unwelcome."[18] There was more work over the summer, some in response to the concerns of campus pastor Martin Wells, who remained a critic of the document.

On 12 October—with a new president in place—the commission brought the second draft of the mission statement to the board of regents. As commission representative, I described the extensive homework involved and the context in which the work was done; multiple crises in higher education, disturbing financial and enrollment problems, and confusion at ELCA headquarters about the nature of the church. (E. Clifford Nelson, the best-known historian of Lutheranism in North America, once remarked that when the ELCA decides what the church is, church colleges can decide what they are.) The commission tried to remain committed to the Lutheran tradition of education and the notions of vocation and service. Themes were paired in a dialectical fashion, reflecting Luther's theological approach: singularity and diversity, liberal arts and professional studies, teaching and research, mind and body (or mind and body and soul), and faith and reason. Academic freedom and loyalty to tradition were also included.

The presentation to the regents ended with several crucial points. First, PLU is a university, not a congregation. A university is not a convent or a seminary, as John Henry Cardinal Newman made clear in his classic *The Idea of a University*; neither is it a Bible college of the contemporary American type marked by fundamentalist triumphalism. Second, PLU is a university in the Lutheran sense with its "two kingdoms" theology, its daring enthusiasm for learning, its sense of vocation and service, and its dedication to academic freedom. Third, PLU is a church-related university, in the current language, of the ELCA. The church and the university have chosen to join together to enhance their common work and concerns, but they are not identical.[19] Regents "commended the committee for their excellent work on the draft statement and appointed four regents to assist them in finalizing the mission statement."[20]

In February 1993 after a two-year gestation, the proposed mission statement was brought to the faculty at its 12 February meeting. It was introduced by a brief statement that summarized the year's revision process and concluded, "We view this statement as an important first step in planning for the future of the university, and challenge the campus community to continue the dialog started through its development."[21] The committee added that because there was concern about "a potential lengthy and confusing process of word smithing by a committee of the whole" it would like action taken without amendments. The motion for the parliamentary suspension of the rules passed. There was a brief statement by committee member Paul Menzel, and I explained committee thinking as I had to the regents. President Anderson—who had inherited the project—spoke in support of the draft. Registrar Charles Nelson moved to refer the document back to the committee. That motion was defeated and the new statement was accepted unanimously.[22] That a university faculty could accept a mission statement unanimously in the early 1990s was a remarkable achievement. It boded well for the future. President Anderson thanked all who had worked on the revised mission statement.

The struggle was not over, however. In the 19 February edition of the *Mast* business professor Glenn Van Wyhe—who had expressed sharp dissatisfaction with the statement on several occasions—submitted a long, heated letter declaring, according to the *Mast* headline, "Jesus left out of PLU's mission statement." The letter was filled with statements taken out of context, careless reasoning, and hyperbole, but it had an impact, especially on some students.[23] The letter focused on the statement's use of the phrase "church-related" rather than "Christian college" and how that usage reflected on whether PLU was Christian.

Van Wyhe's concerns had been addressed in remarks to both regents and faculty. The draft statement and the historical sketch meant to precede it in the university catalog explained at length what "church-related" meant and why it was being used. In the 26 February *Mast* I responded to Van Wyhe's letter at some length and concluded that "to infer from this usage that Christianity is being eliminated from PLU is quite simply absurd."[24]

At a student congregation retreat the weekend after the 12 February faculty meeting three first-year students reacted to the charges in the Van Wyhe letter. (They had not otherwise been involved in discussions, nor had they spoken with any committee members.) They drafted a petition to the board urging a slowdown in the approval process. Other students signed on.

The board met on 21 and 22 February and considered the recommendation from President Anderson "that the Pacific Lutheran University Board of Regents adopt the revised university mission statement as outlined in the attached document."[25] After an hour-long debate the board chose not to do so, but did not explain why. The board moved to thank the committee and instructed the administration, committee, and student leaders to organize a series of public forums and report back to the board on 3 May. The motion passed 14-11.[26]

The spring was filled with forums for students and alumni, letters in the *Mast*, and letters to the president. In response to some of those letters the president wrote:

> Our effort to update the mission statement has been led by a university faculty committee. This committee has worked in concert with the campus community, officials from the Evangelical Lutheran Church in America's Division for Higher Education, Region I church leaders, and members of the Board of Regents. The resulting draft has been approved by the faculty and, according to ELCA officials, clearly affirms the ELCA Division for Higher Education's own understanding of mission for our church colleges and universities. Mission statement writers drew heavily from Martin Luther's call to "serve God and the world" and to educate the whole person—mind, body, and spirit. PLU is committed to the faith development of students and to sustaining a vital and lively religious life on campus.

Professor Glenn Van Wyhe's letter represents one voice in the dialogue. His letter, in my opinion, does not accurately reflect the spirit, intent or content of the proposed mission statement. PLU's proposed mission statement is at the heart of the Lutheran tradition of education.[27]

At the 3 May regents' meeting the proposed mission statement was accepted as a "working document" to serve as a guide and to be studied further in the context of the *PLU 2000* planning process. It was moved and approved "that the draft be viewed as a working document and not be published in the catalog as the mission statement of the university."[28]

The committee and much of the faculty felt blindsided by the board's action. There had been no hint of concern and suggested changes during the conversations of the previous year. What motivated the February and May actions was not clear and, as in the Hunthausen controversy, the board provided no explanation. The draft slid into limbo. The vital importance of such a statement for planning, accreditation, and student service spelled out by President Rieke in April 1991 was lost. And the importance of such a statement, unanimously approved, for faculty selection and activity was lost as well. Those were serious and frustrating matters at an important transformative time in PLU's history, with a new president and long-range planning under way.

Interestingly and ironically, some of the statement's meaning was saved, especially because of the energy and communication skills of the new president. In his written and spoken descriptions of PLU and its mission, Anderson utilized themes in the tradition of Lutheran higher education, especially vocation and service, that had also been captured in the draft statement. In addition, the crucial sentence at the end of the statement's first paragraph was much quoted and soon made its way onto the university's stationery: "The university empowers its students for lives of thoughtful inquiry, service, leadership, and care—for other persons, for the community, and for the earth."[29] That language and those themes also influenced the description of PLU's mission in the long-range planning documents *PLU 2000* and *PLU 2010*, and they soon appeared in various explanations of the university by faculty, staff, and students. The energy expended, the dialogue engendered, and the themes captured in the mission statement had a powerful and positive impact on the university, but the statement itself is still in official board-mandated exile.

THE SUPER COMMITTEE

The selection of a new president did not solve the financial problems that had plagued the university for the previous three years. On 27 April 1992 the board announced that the low bidder for the Mary Baker Russell Music Center was the

Absher Construction Company ($11,245,000), but a $545,000 shortfall remained between the bid price and budgeted cost. The board said negotiations should be used to bridge the gap. President-elect Anderson recommended that a contract not be signed until necessary funding was in place; that advice was not taken.

In October President Anderson told the regents of a "discouraging discovery . . . [of] significant problem areas in the 1992-93 operating budget. It appears we are facing a budget deficit for the current year."[30] In the construction of the budget, problems had been wallpapered over. President Rieke's announcement a year earlier that the university was back in the black and was stronger now sounded tinny.

At the end of August Vice President Don Sturgill had announced his resignation. A national search for his successor was quickly launched. In January the executive committee of the board was told Don Sturgill had "relinquished his remaining duties as vice president for finance and operations and treasurer . . . effective 1 January 1993."[31] Jan Rutledge was appointed acting vice president and President Anderson had to become deeply involved in the intricate details of university finance.

In February William Frame was named vice president for finance and operations. He began work on 1 March. The former treasurer of the Tonka Corporation, he had worked eight years as vice president and senior corporate banker for the First National Bank of Chicago. Frame had a Ph.D. degree in political science from the University of Washington, and he had taught political science at Kenyon College for fourteen years. He said he was "eager to return to academe and to serve in a position that uses all my career experiences."[32] He described himself as reflective, collegial, loyal, and tenacious. All his career experiences were soon at work.

The 1992-93 budget had been balanced by unrealistic revenue assumptions. A $1 million deficit was projected by the end of fiscal year 1993. The situation was explained to the PLU community with candor and the exacting steps taken—embargo on expenditures, layoffs, reorganization—were accepted as necessary. President Anderson's candor significantly strengthened confidence in the new administration. The board encouraged the reform, and its members were drawn into the financial and structural realities of the university in a new way. The board's acceptance of reform was crucially important to its success, and board encouragement, especially by the officers, helped sustain President Anderson and the newly appointed vice president in a demanding situation.[33]

The most immediate financial reform needed was a restructured university balance sheet by means of which the accumulated deficit of the recent past ($4.5 million) could be eliminated. Vice President Frame said some years later:

The basic maneuver for the purpose of restructuring was to re-issue our existing debt at more favorable terms of rate and maturity. To accomplish this we had to make ourselves credit worthy in the estimate of such credit-rating agencies as Moody's and Standard and Poor's. We determined that our revitalization of the university from a financial point of view could not progress fast enough to enable us to refinance our debt on our own recognizance. We turned to a quasi-government agency known as Connie Mae, and asked them to guarantee our debt to public investors with their AAA rating.[34]

Connie Mae agreed for two reasons: a board-led drive to remove about $150,000 of deficit from the unexpended plant fund, and evidence of improving operating efficiencies and rising revenues from new programs. Connie Mae provided the insurance, and the strain on cash flow was reduced. Frame said it also "freed us from the stigma of financial crisis in the mind of the banking community and (most significantly) in the university community itself."[35] The sigh of relief at the university was palpable.

More still had to be done to reduce costs, however. In January the provost, responding to a directive from the president, called together a "super committee" to discuss options and make recommendations about faculty size and academic programs. The committee included all members of the educational policies committee, the rank and tenure committee, and the faculty affairs committee. The committee was officially called the Task Force on Reshaping and Restructuring the Academic Programs at PLU, but unofficially it continued to be called the "super committee." Its work was to end in April, but dragged on beyond that.

In February Project Focus was announced. It was a year-long series of studies and actions aimed at enhancing revenue and reducing costs. The actions allowed savings and reallocations that totaled approximately $1.7 million and balanced the budget. The next phase was announced in June. It included plans for revenue enhancement, less use of part-time faculty, fewer sabbatical replacements, and fewer full-time faculty and staff. It was hoped these actions would produce an additional saving of $1.3 million.[36] The university ended the year in the black, which helped with debt reduction and the rearrangement of debt payment with the Student Loan Marketing Association (Sallie Mae). The university soon negotiated a new interest rate to save as much as five hundred thousand dollars a year, a saving that could be used for other projects. President Anderson and Vice President Frame were very busy.

The various actions and reforms of 1993 brought balanced budgets in 1993-94 and 1994-95. Financial commitments were met, but to move successfully into the last part of the decade additional curricular adjustments and the reduction of approximately fourteen faculty positions were needed. That reduction would save eight hundred thousand dollars and put the university financially "on course." To accomplish that saving, the drastic step of convening the Faculty Joint Committee on Reduction and Reallocation in Force was initiated in March 1995 to continue the Project Focus restructuring process begun two years earlier. Legislation to establish this committee and its procedures was passed by the faculty and approved by the board in 1978, ensuring that if a "financial exigency" emerged the faculty would participate in the reduction and reallocation of faculty positions. "Financial exigency" was defined as a "demonstrably bona fide situation in which the university faces an imminent financial crisis which threatens the survival of the institution as a whole and which cannot reasonably be alleviated by less drastic means than those covered in these policies and procedures."[37] The painful history of such retrenchment at many institutions in the past decade testifies to the wisdom of the 1978 legislation.

April was filled with intense activity. The Deans' Council drew up a series of proposals; faculty, students, and academic units responded; and the provost and joint committee presented their recommendations to the president. He in turn reported to the board. As the activities of April were launched the president told the faculty:

> We are a strong university, with (1) a vital mission and now sharper focus, (2) outstanding faculty and students, (3) properly growing enrollments, (4) and an energetic and ambitious restructuring needed for us to invest properly in our academic future. Thank you for your dedicated work, for your attention to the current matter, and for your forthcoming contributions to our institutional decision-making process.[38]

The joint committee submitted its recommendations in May; they were supported by the provost in August, and approved by the faculty in November. They included: (1) eliminating two master's degree programs in the social sciences, (2) eliminating master's degree programs in physical education and computer science, (3) eliminating a bachelor of science degree program in electrical engineering, and (4) reducing the legal studies program from a major to a minor. The board approved these changes on 27 January 1996.[39] The decisions had been painful, but the entire university community had been involved, guided by legislation passed by both faculty and board more than twenty years before it was needed. Rule of law triumphed.

Linda Hanson studied these events and this process in her 1999 Seattle University doctoral dissertation. The study explained

> how PLU faculty functioned in the collaboration and shared governance with the administration to realign the university's academic programs, restore financial health, and further its mission and purpose. The case, on the whole, counters the prevailing theory in the literature that faculty are not significantly

involved in leading change and demonstrates the circumstances under which faculty resist change . . . While faculty at PLU did not initiate the restructuring project, the dynamic interaction among leaders from faculty and administration formed the leadership imperative that has returned PLU to financial health and restored hope for its future.[40]

Hanson discussed her methodology and conclusions in a presentation at PLU on 27 May 1999. The reallocation process and its decisions were not only described but humanized in her study. President Anderson told her:

> I can't tell you there was a day back in 1992-93 where I sat down at the desk and said, Gee, we need four strategies here. You do what you have to do. Enrollment is down, gosh, better do something. Running a deficit several years? Better fix it. And so you sort of stumble into a set of strategies. When you are new . . . it's not a terribly analytical process in terms of how you're responding.

Hanson summarized the work of the joint committee and its determination to listen carefully, and she described the planning document created by the Dean's Council as not simply "some bureaucratic thing imposed from on high. These were colleagues in a particular role and with certain responsibilities and certain filters for . . . interpreting things, making decisions, but they were also faculty colleagues." The dissertation concluded that the desired outcomes of the restructuring were achieved, but Hanson warned that the study depended on the memory of key informants and was "not generalizeable to other independent universities, beyond PLU."[41] The stalwarts who drafted the faculty constitution in the 1960s and wrote the legislation of 1978 would undoubtedly reply that yes, democracy is clumsy and slow, but it's still the best form of government there is and it can work in lots of institutional settings.

The Mary Baker Russell Music Center

Music department facilities were first-class by the standards of the day when the Chapel-Music-Speech (CMS) building opened in 1952. As the years passed, however, those facilities began to deteriorate and space became a problem as the department grew. Acoustics in the auditorium were always problematic. The need for new facilities was apparent by the late 1960s, but other needs and projects kept crowding out a new music building. Finally, as the centerpiece of the $30 million "Shaping Tomorrow" centennial campaign, a $5.5 million music building was planned. A $1.8 million gift from Tacoma philanthropists Mary Baker Russell and Elbert Baker II in the spring of 1990 launched the campaign. It was decided the building would be called the Mary Baker Russell Music Center.

By the time ground breaking took place on 10 September, the price had risen to $8.9 million. President Rieke announced that construction would begin in the winter and the building would be finished by September 1993. When the bidding process was completed, on 27 April 1992, the price had risen to more than $11 million and not all the money was available. President-elect Anderson advised delay until the money was either pledged or in-hand, but the contract was signed with the Absher Construction Company by board chair Wold and Vice President Sturgill.

Environmental concerns were raised over the summer by campus environmental activists—the Dirt People—and the Pierce County Audubon Society. They objected to the proposed removal of eight rare Oregon white oaks on the hillside construction site. Less than a week before the mitigation deadline one of those campus activists, Jeanette Dorner, walked into the Pierce County Planning Department with a $350 filing fee and an appeal about the proposed mitigation for the building. She said, "I know what this means to the university, but it was too important to let go."[42] It meant environmental investigation, but also delay and increased costs. President Anderson expressed exasperation, but he was also ambivalent. The delay would allow more opportunity for fundraising.

On 4 November 1992 an open forum was held to discuss the environmental issues, and a committee was formed to discuss concerns about the building's hillside location. The possibility of moving the building fifty feet east to preserve trees soon emerged. In December Dorner's appeal to the county was denied, but discussion of finances continued. The architects were asked to consider a phased construction of the building. If that was possible, construction could begin in 1993. In April the decision was made to move the building fifty-one feet east and fourteen feet south and to plan for phased construction. Phase one would include the concert hall, classrooms, and practice space; phase two would include rehearsal rooms, practice studios, faculty offices, and administrative space. Its construction would depend on additional funding.

With gifts from Mary Baker Russell (who gave the project $4.5 million over the years), George Lagerquist (whose generosity funded the concert hall), and a plethora of additional donors, the first phase of the Mary Baker Russell Music Center was finished and dedicated on 3 February 1995. The entire weekend was filled with concerts. Excitement and gratitude filled the new building. Designed by Zimmer Gunsul Frasca Partnership, the building had a European style entrance designed to heighten the anticipation of concert goers as they entered. To their left on the east windows hung the remarkable Dale Chihuly glass sculpture. The 534-seat Lagerquist Concert Hall was shaped in a traditional shoebox fashion. It was finished in one-hundred-year-old wheat-colored fir, a tribute to Lagerquist's lifelong work in the timber industry. The walls were split-face concrete blocks with alternating rough and smooth sides to improve sound quality. The carpet, concrete flooring, and seats all helped shape sound. To fine-tune acoustics, red velour banners hung on the room's sides could be raised or lowered depending on the type of music played. Orchestra director Jerry Kracht claimed he "heard the orchestra for the first time in twenty five years." In Eastvold "the low notes used to rumble along without definition, direction, or purpose; they soar cleanly in the new concert hall. The room works with us."[43] The first orchestral selection played was Beethoven's "Consecration of the House Overture." The work was designed to test the acoustics of a room; the orchestra plays three chords, each followed by a pause, to hear what the room gives back. The room responded perfectly.

Money for the internationally famous glass artist Dale Chihuly's sculpture hung inside the east windows was given by George Lagerquist. He wanted Chihuly's work to celebrate PLU's central icon, the Eastvold rose window. The four pieces were also influenced by Martin Luther's rose. Luther described his rose in this way:

> First there is a black cross set in a heart of natural color to remind me that faith in the Crucified One saves us. . . . Even though it is a black cross, one that mortifies the flesh and should produce pain, it leaves the color of the heart intact, does not destroy our nature, that is, it does not kill but preserves life. . . . The heart is mounted in the center of a white rose to show that faith brings joy, comfort, and peace. . . . Since the peace and joy are unlike that of the world, the rose is white and not red, for white is the color of spirits and angels.

The Chihuly roses are hung on aluminum frames; there are four banks of "spinners," or glass discs that swirl lightly upward like sea shells. They are red, blue, green, and white. Chihuly had never used white before on the edges of the "spinners," nor had he crafted symbolism into them. The green rose symbolized God the creator. It contains the first letter of the Hebrew word for God, Yahweh, and its color suggests the evergreen beauty of the Northwest. The blue rose (the dominant color of the Eastvold rose window) has three entwined rings symbolizing the Trinity. It points to baptismal water and eternity. The white rose captures themes in Luther's rose, and the red rose symbolizes Jesus the Christ. It reflects sacrifice, passion, and the Holy Spirit. The Chihuly roses mark the entrance to the music center in a dramatic way.

When planning and fundraising for the music center began it did not seem possible that an organ could be included in the budget, but a $250,000 gift from Jeff and Patty Smith (Jeff Smith was the Frugal Gourmet of public television fame) turned thinking around. The naming gift of $300,000 came from the Gottfried and Mary Fuchs Foundation. Additional gifts from Mary Baker Russell, the Lutheran Brotherhood Insurance Company, and many others boosted the fund total. The northern European-style mechanical action organ was built by the Paul Fritts and Co. Organ Builders. Fritts is the son of Jean (a 1952 alumna) and R. Byard Fritts, a PLU music department faculty member from 1949 to 1966. Paul Fritts grew up in Parkland, where his shop is located. He has an international reputation. Fritts spent 300 hours on his computer planning the organ and building took more than 24,000 hours. Fritts has called the Fuchs organ his "magnum opus." It is actually four organs, each with its own keyboard and pipes and distinct sounds and purposes. The organ is 34 feet high and 27 feet wide, with 3,700 pipes. The case carvings were done by Fritts's sister, Judy Fritts. The total cost was $920,000. Music department chair David Robbins, who played a significant role in the planning and construction of the music building, proclaimed the completion of the organ "a magnificent accomplishment." University organist David Dahl called it the "dream of a lifetime for an organist. All the components of the finest organs in history are here."[44] The organ preview celebration took place on 2 April 1997.

Ground breaking for the second phase of the music center construction occurred in December 1996. It was the result of two unexpected gifts from Mary Baker Russell. President Anderson reported: "The university's capacity to move forward with this project is made possible by Mary Baker Russell's generosity, vision, and commitment to our students and our music program. I hope you will join me in celebrating this good news and expressing the thanks of a grateful university to Mary Baker Russell."[45]

Mary Baker Russell died on 14 August 1997 at the age of 89. Three days before her death she set up an $800,000 music scholarship program. Chairs at the front of the concert hall are permanently assigned to George Lagerquist and Mary Baker Russell. Their generosity transformed the study and performance of music at Pacific Lutheran University.

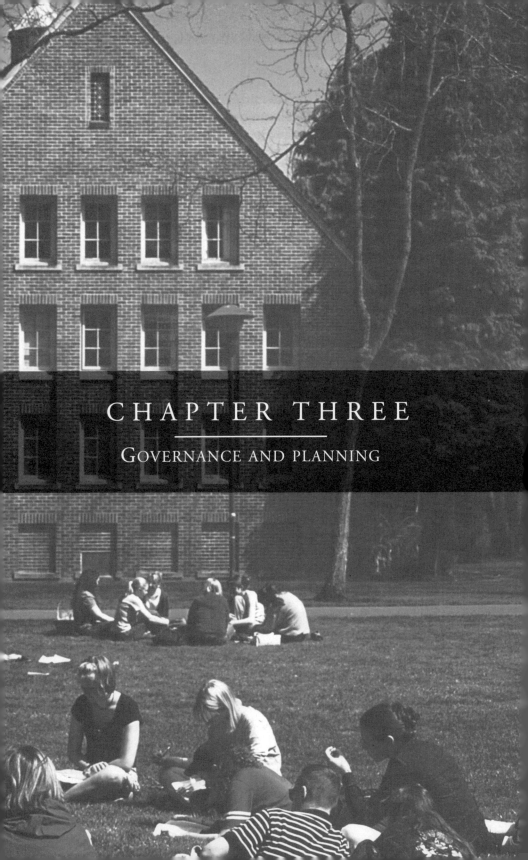

CHAPTER THREE

GOVERNANCE AND PLANNING

Chapter Three

GOVERNANCE AND PLANNING

IN THE MIDST OF THE PRESSURES, problems, and actions of the early 1990s, campus and academic life flourished. Student accomplishments were noteworthy. In April 1994 it was announced that Jennifer Dyer had won a Goldwater scholarship, granted by the federal government to subsidize research for especially able science students. One year earlier Jennifer Specht had similarly won a Goldwater scholarship, as had Tom Kaneko two years before. All three later attended medical school. Dyer (Dietrich) is now an obstetrician-gynecologist, Specht-Brannfors is a cancer researcher, and Kaneko is a medical school teacher. In May it was announced that campus environmental activist Jeanette Dorner had won a Fulbright scholarship. She planned to study Indian ecosystems at the Center for International Studies of Mountain and Hill Environments at the University of Delhi. She was also interested in learning more about Indian culture and getting to know her Indian relatives.

In December the *Mast* included a long supplement on the alcohol policy at PLU, entitled "Old Policy, New Times." Thoughtful and well written, it continued an editorial preoccupation dating back to the 1960s: "While most aspects of student life have changed in the past 100 years, PLU's alcohol policy hasn't. Is it past its time?" There were articles about PLU, comparisons with Seattle Pacific University and Lewis and Clark College, and a discussion of the influence of federal standards. Rules against dancing and smoking on campus have fallen, the *Mast* concluded, but the alcohol policy remains.[1]

Faculty achievements and activities were also noteworthy, and some intersected with world affairs. In June 1992 economics professor Stanley Brue visited Moscow at the joint invitation of Moscow State University and the American embassy in Moscow, to present the first week of a three-week demonstration course on the principles of market economics. About fifty Russian professors participated. Brue's invitation arose from his co-authorship with C. R. McConnell of *Economics* (then in its twelfth edition), the best-selling introductory economics textbook in the United States, which had just been translated and published in Russia. Anatoly Porokhov, director of the translation, reported that one million students would use the book the following academic year and five hundred thousand copies had been printed. Russia was moving its economics curriculum from "Marx to markets" in one year, and the Brue-McConnell textbook was to play a major role in the transition.[2]

Also in 1992, retired accounting professors Eldon Schafer and Dwight Zulauf taught accounting in a summer session at Riga Technical University in the Latvian capital. Their two-week workshop, "Accounting in a Market Economy," was part of an "entrepreneurial summer school" sponsored by the U.S. Information Agency in cooperation with PLU. Participants "learned about the role of managerial accounting in decision making and performance evaluation."[3] Schafer and Zulauf also taught managerial accounting workshops for several years to groups of Russians brought to PLU by 1969 graduate James Ojala, who was active organizing education workshops and exchanges for Russians in the 1990s.

Still in 1992, physics professor K. T. Tang received the prestigious Humboldt Research Award for senior U.S. scientists. Tang was nominated for the award by Dr. Jan-Peter Toennies, director of the Max Planck Institute in Gottingen, Germany. Toennies noted that "according to international standards, Tang is one of the best known theoreticians in the fields of dynamics of reaction processes and intermolecular interactions." The award entitled Tang to stay for twelve months at the Max Planck Institute and carry out research of his choice. Since coming to PLU in 1967 Tang has published more than one hundred papers; in all of them, Toennies said, "Tang has understood how to develop new, original ideas and to bring them to fruition."

In November award-winning writer and English professor Jack Cady published his eighth book, *The Sons of Noah and Other Stories*. All his works have a common theme, Cady explained—doing the right thing in the context of the character's particular situations—but they have no central message. Readers should find their own messages. He felt that experience was the only way to learn how to be a writer.

Music professor David Hoffman was also very much in the news, in a non-academic way. Despite thirty years of mountain climbing experience, he fell fourteen hundred feet down Alaska's Mt. McKinley in a climbing accident. "We were working conservatively, but the mountain spat back at us," he recalled. A sheet of ice gave way and he "expected one of the slams to kill me." He said he would climb again when his injuries healed.[4]

Faculty Governance

In the spring of 1991 faculty concerns about its system of governance produced an ad hoc committee designed to investigate the processes of governance and suggest improvements.[5] The central theme of the 1991 faculty fall conference, chief concerns were the relative ineffectiveness of the committee system and, as the committee reported, the "faculty's role in its own affairs and in those affairs of the university which were of legitimate interest to the faculty had been seriously degraded, perhaps necessitating a change in the basic structure of faculty governance."[6] The committee suggested two models: one proposed moderate change, retaining the faculty assembly and adding a faculty chair and executive committee; the other proposed more radical change with a faculty senate as the core of the system. Both models included reform of the committee system. The faculty approved the more moderate model, affirming an essentially collegial form of governance.

The core of the revision was creation of faculty officers (a faculty chair, vice chair, and secretary), and an executive committee. In addition to conducting faculty assembly and executive committee meetings, the chair provided a focal point for faculty representation to and from the administration.[7] The chair would receive a two-course release (one-third of an annual teaching load) and serve two years. The executive committee was composed of the faculty officers, chairs of the standing committees, an elected representative, and the university president and provost. It was designed to coordinate the work of faculty committees, help prepare the agenda for faculty meetings, and provide oversight for ad hoc committees. Committees and committee functions were consolidated when possible and feasible; little structural change was produced for major committees, but the number of standing committees was reduced from eighteen to nine. The most substantial consolidation brought seven committees under the umbrella of the new campus life committee. The new governance committee replaced the former committee on committees and judiciary committee. After votes on nineteen resolutions to make the appropriate constitutional, by-laws, and faculty handbook changes, the reformed system of governance was launched in September 1993.

The new system, while not perfect, was a marked improvement, and faculty business was facilitated more effectively. The faculty chair spoke formally during the fall conference, laying out an agenda for the year, and the executive committee brought greater focus and coordination to committee activity. Regular conversations between the president, provost, and faculty chair clarified issues and actions in a helpful way. President Rieke's concern about sovereignty and President Anderson's fear that transferring responsibility for chairing faculty meetings to a faculty member might seem a demotion for a new president turned out to be non-issues. It was helpful rather than a diminution of power for the president to be able to listen, reflect, and speak when appropriate and necessary. Parliamentary restrictions on the president's ability to speak on agenda items when presiding, an issue since the 1940s and occasionally ignored, were now lifted for the president but applied to the faculty chair.[8]

PLU 2000

Pacific Lutheran University has engaged in serious long-range planning at various times in its history. A comprehensive academic and physical plan was produced by the end of the 1920s but undermined by the Great Depression. The present campus configuration was largely produced by a series of plans drafted in the mid-1960s. By the 1980s the board of regents began to push hard for more careful and comprehensive planning, and faculty and administration responded with various degrees of enthusiasm. Faculty efforts were often utopian—presidential candidate Ryan Amacher described the plan he saw in 1991 as a "wish list"—and administrative muscle was rarely used to bring the plans to earth. Many thought it was more important to be able to respond quickly to curricular and programmatic possibilities in the fluid and entrepreneurial 1980s. Despite significant faculty, staff, curricular, and programmatic growth during the decade, planning was not very successful and growth often lacked direction.

By the end of the decade serious problems began to appear in higher education, both locally and nationally. The problems were complex, but primarily financial and demographic in nature. Whether they were addressed early enough at PLU is a moot question. After President William Rieke announced his retirement, the presidential search was guided by a carefully constructed "needs analysis." All the constituent groups that shaped the document emphasized the crucial importance of long-range planning and fundraising skills in the next president. Planning began quickly after President Anderson took office.

The process that launched *PLU 2000: Embracing the 21st Century—The Long-Range Plan of Pacific Lutheran University* began in December 1992 with the appointment of a long-range planning committee by President Anderson. The committee's charge was to identify the themes to be addressed as the university moved into the twenty-first century. Provost J. Robert Wills and associate dean of nursing Carolyn Schultz accepted the responsibility of orchestrating the drafting of a planning document. (Wills resigned in 1993 and was replaced by vice president of finance and operations William Frame). The eight study commissions that emerged—composed of faculty, staff, and students—produced forty-two "issue papers" that guided campus discussions during the 1993-94 academic year. Final reports were submitted by the early summer of 1994, and a draft was completed during the summer and discussed the next fall. Final acceptance by the faculty and board was completed by January 1995. The board "enthusiastically" approved the plan. *PLU 2000* decisively shaped the next five years.

The plan was divided into three parts. Part I, "Industry Trends and Competitive Factors," set the stage for the rest of the document. It discussed national and regional educational trends, the growth reversal at PLU, and "the University Today." It concluded that recent enrollment and financial reversals "wounded" the institution but did not "cripple" it, because PLU was perceived as providing "(1) an education which takes matters of value and faith seriously, in (2) a core array of programs linked to occupational demands, and (3) offered by a vibrant faculty . . . accessible to students." Planning, careful stewardship of resources, and extending PLU's tradition were all necessary to move into the twenty-first century in good order.

Part II of *PLU 2000* laid out the consensus platform for action. It was made up of five axioms: (1) a series of proposals gathered under the title of "Strengthening The Learning Community"; (2) reaffirmation of the university's participation in the tradition of Lutheran higher education; (3) adoption of "education for lives of service" as PLU's motto and statement of educational purposes; (4) development of a more diverse community; and (5) means for supporting the enterprise. Each axiom was described in some detail.

Part III, "The *PLU 2000* Action Plan: Authorized Initiatives," laid out twenty-two initiatives designed to define and realize the implications of Part II's axioms. For example, initiatives for "Strengthening The Learning Community" included "Academic Excellence," "Public Discourse," "The New American College," "Program Assessment," "Excellence in Scholarship," and "Eliminating Obstacles." All twenty-two initiatives were seriously addressed in the next several years, with remarkable success. The administration was serious about keeping the plan in sharp focus and measuring results.

PLU 2000 concluded with a message from President Anderson. He thanked those who participated in creating the plan and asked, what finally is PLU about? His response cited language from the plan itself: "One sentence . . . better than any other single statement, points us to our future: 'PLU seeks to empower students for lives of thoughtful inquiry, leadership, service and care—for other people, for their communities, and for the earth.'" He added: "Our next round of planning begins at this point."[9]

In 1997, in response to the specific challenge to build a more distinguished and distinctive academic program, two emphases were added to *PLU 2000*: active learning and integration of the liberal arts and professional education. They were described in some detail and added to the twenty-two initiatives already on the agenda.

CHANGE

In December 1993 provost and communications professor J. Robert Wills announced his retirement effective 31 May. He said he wanted to return to the classroom. "I had known for a long time that I wasn't going to make central administration my career." Theatre professor William Becvar said he wasn't prepared to comment on the role Wills might play in the department, though he was pleased with Wills's qualifications. While serving as provost Wills had directed two plays.[10]

The search for a new provost was quickly launched. Despite more than one hundred applicants by May, no appointment was made. Philosophy professor Paul Menzel agreed to serve in an interim capacity. Another search was launched in the fall; it too was unsuccessful and in February 1995 Menzel agreed to serve for three years. Paul Menzel was a 1964 graduate of the College of Wooster, with a B.D. degree from Yale University and a Ph.D. degree from Vanderbilt University. Interested in philosophical ethics, he had recently written extensively about health care decision making. Although he had not been a candidate for the full-time position and would rather teach and do research, the search committee made an offer he had not expected: four to six weeks off each summer for scholarly study. He agreed to serve for three years, focusing especially on Project Focus, *PLU 2000*, and New American College activities. He said, "I'm not changing careers."[11]

There were additional resignations and a retirement during this same period. In February vice president for church relations Harvey Neufeld retired after twenty-seven years of service. He described his job as a "keeper of memories." His book about his extensive travels, *Traveling with Harv*, was published by the PLU Press. In April campus pastors Susan Briehl and Martin Wells announced they had accepted a position as executive directors of Holden Village, the Lutheran retreat center in the Cascade mountains above Lake Chelan. In February 1995 the third member of the campus ministry, Dan Erlander, "waved good-bye" to PLU and a campus "filled with wonderful people and friendships." He would serve as a part-time pastor on Whidbey Island and continue to write and illustrate his unique and widely used books. The three had been energetic and creative campus pastors.

HARMONY

In September 1993 English professor Tom Campbell and history professor Beth Kraig made a "difficult, but necessary decision" leading to two announcements. They announced the organization of Harmony, a group formed to discuss issues of sexual orientation, and on a more personal level they chose to disclose to the PLU community that they were homosexual. Professor Kraig was a candidate for tenure, and she wanted all facts on the table before those considerations began. Harmony would be open to all students and would be organized differently than Crossroads, a group that had been meeting confidentially to discuss sexual orientation. Harmony would have open meetings, with hopes that civility would prevail and courtesy for all views would prevail. Campbell and Kraig wrote that Harmony was looking for ideas, respect, and good neighbors.[12] The first meeting drew a positive response, approximately eighty people, and more questions than answers.

Letters about Harmony and its discussions soon began pouring into the

Mast's offices. On 1 October they were supportive; on 8 October they were more critical. One student urged obeying the Word of God and discerning God's position. Business professor Glenn Van Wyhe wrote that we must love the sinner but hate the sin and call the sinner away from sin. That call may sometimes be harsh, he conceded, "but only a person who cares nothing for Jesus would use his name to support a violation of the holiness to which He called us."[13] On 15 October four letters warned against inappropriate and uninformed judgment. By November civility still ruled Harmony meetings and faculty and administration were supportive; reaction from outside the university had been minimal.

In November 1994 the campus united in response to hate mail. Four students had received letters expressing views of racism, anti-feminism, and homophobia from persons identifying themselves as the PLU Ku Klux Klan. President Anderson and Vice President Erv Severtson wrote a letter to the campus community affirming PLU's values, condemning the letters, and offering a five-hundred-dollar reward for identifying the letter writers. Campus Safety and the Pierce County Sheriff's office were soon involved; those responsible faced possible criminal charges related to malicious harassment. Severtson called the letters "de-humanizing, ugly, and disturbing." They had been received by an African-American, an Asian-American, and a senior student who was coordinating a diversity forum. The fourth recipient was not identified. In December one of the four students admitted he had written a second letter to himself. He thought not enough was being done about diversity and wanted to make that clear; he said he didn't write the first four letters. He was expelled.[14]

Harmony meetings continued to be well attended, but issues related to sexual orientation were stirred up dramatically in the spring of 1996 by several editorials written by the *Mast* editor, Lindsay Tomac. They elicited more heated response than any issue since those of the 1960s.

The first editorial was entitled "Homosexual supporters losing sight of people focus." She argued that under the guise of diversity people involved with homosexual organizations had been "charging up students" with their messages through programs. "Personally, I believe homosexuality is immoral. The Bible states that homosexuality should not be practiced." Hatred was also wrong, she wrote, but "since I accept the Bible at the literal level, the ethics of the issue are clear to me." Tomac supported diversity, but not when it was "stretched to mean that we must accept the lifestyle of an individual when it goes against our conscience and beliefs." She said she had been "accosted" by many and accused of hate, fear, and ignorance, but she could not change her views. The focus of diversity should be accepting people, not all beliefs and lifestyles. Tomac concluded that all the homosexual-based programs sponsored by PLU created an atmosphere where people no longer feel comfortable voicing their beliefs for fear of condemnation. "In the past it was the homosexuals who feared condemnation.

Now the tables have been turned and our focus has been lost."[15]

There was much response to the editorial from a variety of perspectives. Tomac said she was surprised at the ease with which some who had no prior knowledge of her judged her character and capacity to love. She was judged by her editorial, not her life example. She had tried to find a middle ground, but the "homosexuals I have spoken to have been unwilling to budge. The message to me has been clear. They insist that the middle ground must be found on their side of the fence."[16]

Most of the student-written letters over the next several weeks were critical of Tomac's position, but a long letter signed by ten people associated with the athletic department, including tennis coach Mike Benson and the three football coaches, Frosty Westering, Scott Westering, and Craig McCord, was supportive. It emphasized that the "Bible is the sole standard of truth and error in Christianity." They affirmed the right of gay pastors and homosexuals who "profess to follow Jesus Christ" to interpret the Bible on these matters, but they urged readers not to "presume that all professing Christians share their same beliefs, for we most assuredly do not." To believe the Bible does not condemn homosexuality in the Body of Christ, they wrote, is a "false representation of scripture."[17]

In the 12 April *Mast* professor Glenn Van Wyhe called for a debate to deal with the "central issue of whether homosexuality is good or bad." He concluded his long letter by asserting that "if God tells us that homosexuality is bad, then it is wise and good not to disagree with Him." In the same issue Brett Johnson, a 1995 graduate, responded to the coaches' letter.

> Football coaches and friends, you need not be afraid of Beth Kraig and other members of the gay community at PLU. Her work does nothing to weaken the Christian stronghold that is the PLU athletic department. But she does provide refuge and guidance to your own student athletes when they cannot turn to you for fear of rejection. Consider her not as the adversarial leader of a rival Christian sect, but as a fellow colleague who is working to help the students for whom this university exists. You should do the same.

The 12 April issue had still more letters, including one from the faculty and staff diversity committee. "Celebrating diversity includes sexual minorities," it asserted. "Lindsay Tomac makes a troubling claim in her first editorial . . . that the 'excessive number of homosexual-based programs' at PLU have served to make heterosexuals uncomfortable—her desire ultimately is voiced as a nostalgia for the days when gay people were closeted, silenced or made otherwise inconspicuous."[18] Religion professor Patricia Killen wrote a long letter about biblical interpretation answering the coaches' missive. She provided a long historical account about how the Bible has been variously interpreted and said the coaches' sole reliance on the Word of God in scripture ignores the Holy Spirit. Moreover, the question is not about opinion but faithful interpretation. The coaches, she warned, "risk falling into Bibliolatry: replacing the worship of God with the worship of the Bible. This is the direction I fear my colleagues' positions lead . . . Those of us who claim to be followers of Jesus should approach the scriptures with care rivaled only by our willingness to call into question our own limited grasp of the truth."[19]

Letters continued until the end of the semester. It was the most heated exchange in several decades. The importance of a university in facilitating such an exchange about such an important matter was made clear once again. Harmony continued to meet and civility at its meetings continued as well.

In September 1996 the *Matrix*, a new literary magazine, appeared. The intent of the editors was to focus on complex social justice issues that were not otherwise adequately dealt with on campus. The first issue addressed "Race, Ethnicity, and Identity." The faculty advisor was Beth Kraig.

HONORS

Honors of various kinds were both given and received in the middle part of the decade. On 26 October 1995 Queen Sonja and King Harald V of Norway visited campus. The queen received a doctorate of humane letters for her commitment to humanitarian concerns, including the Red Cross, international refugees, and disabled children. The royal couple was on a month-long tour of the United States. A year later, famed explorer Thor Heyerdahl received the President's Medal for his achievements, offering a public lecture and book signing during his visit. PLU graduate and humanities fellow Donald Ryan, who was serving as Heyerdahl's personal assistant, was instrumental in bringing him to campus.

In March 1996 it was announced that Paul Hoseth would replace David Olson as athletic director and dean of the School of Physical Education. Olson had served twenty-eight years and "built one of the most successful small college athletic programs in the country."[20] Hoseth, a Concordia College graduate who had joined the PLU faculty in 1968, was described by the *Mast* as a "veteran newcomer." He said his primary interest in the position was in the program's philosophical approach that wrapped athletics and academics tightly together, thanks largely to Olson's efforts. The success of that philosophy, Olson's leadership, coaches' commitment, and athletes' enthusiasm was dramatically realized when PLU was awarded the Sears Directors' Cup in 1996. The Directors' Cup is the ultimate collegiate athletic award because it honors institutions with broad-based athletic programs that include a range of sports. PLU was best in the 400-member National Association of Intercollegiate Athletics for the 1995-96 academic year. Criteria considered included competition in both men's and women's sports; PLU had no national championship teams that year but several teams and individuals competing at the national level to win. Winners in other divisions included Stanford University, the University of California at Davis, and Williams College.

In November the *Mast* announced that twenty-two-year-old Calvin Goings, a 1995 political science graduate, had become the youngest state senator in Washington state history. "I really believe, and I know it sounds kind of corny," he commented, "that when people get involved they can still make a difference."

AFTER FIVE YEARS

The first five years of Loren Anderson's presidency were intensely busy. They were filled with difficulties—some unexpected—but the difficulties were wrestled down and the achievements were significant. By 1997 the institution was nicely situated to enter the new millennium. Anderson acknowledged assistance from the president's council, adding that "we have a strong leadership group, but way beyond that PLU is blessed with incredibly gifted and dedicated faculty and staff . . . the growth and well being of our students is their primary focus and they regularly give service above and beyond the call of duty. They are the well-spring of PLU's excellence."[21] The board began to play a more active role in PLU's financial and development life as well. Anderson wanted an active, informed, and generous board; he worked hard to bring that about.

Achievements of the five-year period include completion of the Mary Baker Russell Music Center with its Lagerquist Concert Hall, Fuchs organ, and Chihuly glass sculpture, all raising the study and performance of music to a new level. The draft mission statement, while not officially embraced, illuminated discussions about PLU's purpose and identity well into the next decade, and the reform of faculty governance was a significant improvement. The Sears Cup was a major honor for the athletic department.

The three major successes of Anderson's first five years were Project Focus, *PLU 2000*, and the "Make a Lasting Difference" fundraising campaign. All were cooperative faculty, staff, and administrative enterprises whose success continues to shape the institution. Project Focus responded to the enrollment and financial difficulties of the early 1990s. Five programs were eliminated to help focus academic effort and resources. With extensive administrative reorganization, over three million dollars was saved for reallocation, and the university's employment was reduced by about ten percent. The operating deficit of $4.3 million was eliminated by 1996, four years earlier than planned. Anderson said: "The strength and courage of the PLU community has been evident throughout this period of economic recovery. All have been willing to sacrifice and, as a result, the university looks forward to a very bright future."[22] The president's candor through all of Project Focus was a constant and positive influence. *PLU 2000*'s statement of institutional vision and identity became the core planning document that guided the university through the rest of the 1990s and beyond. The university worked hard to reach its axioms' goals.

Perhaps the most dramatic success of this period was the "Make A Lasting Difference" fundraising campaign chaired by 1960 graduate Donald R. Morken, chair and CEO of Genesee Investments. He was assisted by a large national campaign cabinet that provided local and national leadership and an energetic development staff. The goal set for the campaign was $52 million; the final result was more than $72 million. It was a liberating triumph. The endowment was raised from $8.2 million to $27 million, a crucial advance. Other advances included the Names Family Endowment for Athletics, the Names Court (a wooden basketball floor in Olson Auditorium), a language resources center, a University Center computer user room, residence hall renovations, classroom upgrades, natural sciences equipment, and a new surface on the running track.

While celebrating these various advances the president also focused on the future. Increasing enrollment and reducing expenses remained paramount, but new plans were being formulated as well: an academic plan, a campus physical master plan, a technology plan, and a financial plan. There would be no resting on laurels. As the president put it:

> The future presents exciting opportunities. We stand on the brink of a new millennium. Our campus was planted on tomorrow's world of the Pacific Rim, and this university can only flourish because of the dedication of a remarkable faculty and staff, and students who yearn to make a difference. God has blessed PLU beyond measure. And to whom much has been given, much is expected.[23]

DRATT NECESS
UT NOT SUFFICIE
AMILY M
TTERS
ORGANIZATIONAL
IC RELATIONS
CONNELL

CHAPTER FOUR

A New Millennium

Chapter Four

A New Millennium

THE LAST PART OF THE 1990S saw much activity on campus, but especially significant was the increased level of faculty and student scholarship. Despite the demands of Project Focus, faculty governance reform, and heavy teaching loads, faculty began producing books and articles with unprecedented regularity, and they attracted notable attention.[1] The scholarly activity of history professor Christopher Browning is the most striking example. An Oberlin graduate with a Ph.D. degree from the University of Wisconsin, Browning was told in graduate school that a specialty in Holocaust studies would be a professional dead end; he disagreed, persevered, and when the field took off a few years later he was in the midst of the most important interpretive debates of the next twenty-five years. At PLU, Holocaust and German history courses were added to the curriculum, and students were caught up in the need to understand the Holocaust, both morally and intellectually.[2]

Browning's dissertation was published in 1978: *The Final Solution and the German Foreign Office*. Articles and books continued to flow from his computer; most important, *Ordinary Men* (1992) rearranged thinking about the Holocaust with its argument that under the right circumstances "ordinary men" became willing executioners, helping the Nazi ideologues commit horrific acts. During his years at PLU Browning won numerous awards, and he was a visiting scholar at the United States Holocaust Memorial Museum, the Institute for Advanced Study on the campus of Hebrew University in Jerusalem, and the Institute for Advanced Study at Princeton. He also taught at Northwestern University and the University of Wisconsin.

In March 1998 Browning gave the twenty-fourth annual Walter Schnackenberg Lecture at PLU to a crowd of more than three hundred. Those attending were met by two protesters at the door who claimed the Holocaust never happened. His speech, "Adolph Hitler and the Decision for the Final Solution: An Old Question and New Documents," described new documents, available after 1989, that had influenced the "intentionalist-functionalist" debate of the previous decade. Browning took a third view, contending that the Final Solution was produced by a series of incremental decisions: Hitler made key decisions between July and October 1941, but they were not premeditated.[3] Browning's influence on this issue was widespread on both sides of the Atlantic.

Browning's international reputation was dramatically evident when he was invited to give the Trevelyan Lectures, probably the most prestigious English language lectureship for historians—at Cambridge University in spring 1999. Only a handful of American historians, none from west of the Mississippi River and none from a small university, had ever been so honored. The lectures were published by Cambridge University Press in 2000. Browning left PLU in 1999, after twenty-five years, to accept the Frank Porter Graham chair in history at the University of North Carolina. He has continued to publish extensively, including his magnum opus, a 615-page, twenty-year project, *The Origins of the Final Solution: The Evolution of Nazi Jewish Policy, September 1939-March 1942*, written as part of the comprehensive History of the Holocaust, organized by the Yad Vashem Society. Browning is the most widely known and influential faculty scholar in the history of PLU.

In November 1998 psychology professor Brian Baird was elected to the United States Congress from Washington's third district. A crucial campaign boost came from the work of eighteen college students who helped with grass roots activity. Baird had taught twelve years at PLU and, after a narrow loss in 1996, was the first faculty member elected to Congress. He said he wanted "to restore reason and moderation to a Congress that is being ruled by partisan decisions," and to be known as a "problem solver."[4]

In March 2001 Richard Sparks resigned his faculty position and directorship of the Choir of the West; he had served since 1983. Founder and director of Choral Arts Northwest, a vocal ensemble of twenty-six voices, and director of Pro Coro Canada, a professional chamber choir based in Edmonton, Alberta, Sparks wanted to spend more time with those groups. The Choir of the West toured Scandinavia in the summer after his resignation and celebrated its seventy-five years of history the following year.

Sparks was succeeded by Kathryn Lehman, a 1975 PLU graduate who had sung in the choir under Maurice Skones; her father had sung under Gunnar Malmin. Her Lehman grandparents had operated a grocery store in Parkland during the 1930s, helping to feed the faculty during the Depression. Lehman said, "I believe I was called to be here. I had a role to play. . . . I feel very strongly about the tradition of music and faith." She told the *Mast* she believed music is about enjoyment and she wanted to teach students how music can enrich their lives. She said she wanted a flexible-sounding choir, able to perform multicultural forms of music, with a bigger, more soloistic style. Lehman had a master's degree in vocal performance and pedagogy from the Westminster Choir College and was a doctoral candidate at the University of Colorado. She had most recently taught at Oregon State University and the University of Oregon. She was only the fifth director of the Choir of the West since its founding in 1927.[5]

In the fall of 1998 three key administrative positions were filled. Donald Bell was hired as the new dean of the school of business. He emphasized re-accreditation and spreading the reputation of the school, and he was intrigued by and wanted to teach in the "critical conversation" portion of the core curriculum. Terry Miller became the new dean in nursing. Educated in Oklahoma and Texas, he had come to PLU after long service at San Jose State University. He promised a new curriculum on the agenda. As the new vice president of Development, David Aubrey, would direct the new $100 million campaign. He had served as a Lutheran pastor and in fundraising for Valparaiso University, Luther Seminary, California Lutheran University, and the American Heart Association.

After only eighteen months of service, Charles Upshaw resigned from the finance and operations vice presidency in the spring of 1999. He was replaced in an acting capacity by chemistry professor Sheri Tonn, an Oregon native, who had joined the faculty in 1979 with a Ph.D. degree from Northwestern University. She had a wealth of experience as department chair, divisional dean, informational resources dean, and as a member of the recent presidential search committee and the mission statement committee. Her appointment was made permanent in February 2000. Tonn's boundless energy was soon released in various directions on a number of projects.

It took a year to replace Erv Severtson as vice president of student life after his 1999 retirement. When the first search failed, *Mast* editor Laura Ritchie wrote that students needed an explanation.[6] The search committee refused, but in February 2000 Laura Majovski received a permanent appointment as vice president. A Duke graduate with a 1982 doctorate from the Graduate School of Psychology at Fuller Theological Seminary, she had worked in PLU's counseling center and as assistant to the president.

ANAC

In April 1999 it was announced that PLU had joined twenty other institutions as a member of the Associated New American Colleges. The organization was formed in 1995 to enable its member institutions—small to mid-sized private comprehensive colleges and universities with student-centered liberal arts and professional missions—to collaborate in advancing teaching and learning. The institutions share a commitment to teaching and scholarship, a collegial ethos centered on students and values, and an effort to integrate liberal and professional education while preserving liberal arts as a core mission. They offer both professional and adult-learner programs, not usually found in liberal arts colleges. Most ANAC members offer some graduate programs.[7] All value scholarship, but in the teacher-scholar faculty model, the primary commitment is to teaching. Members included two other Lutheran institutions, Susquehana University and Valparaiso University, and two other west coast institutions, Saint Mary's College and the University of Redlands.

The ANAC schools' determination to integrate liberal and professional learning was similar to recent attempts at PLU to deal with those issues, energized by Project Focus. The struggle dated back to the origin of the university and periodically produced a dissonance or ambivalence that made explaining or defining identity and purpose problematic. It was hoped that ANAC membership would help produce a clearer sense of purpose and identity. Interesting evidence suggests some of that is happening today: in various departmental curricular revisions, the results of Project Focus; the First-Year Experience Program; attempts to hammer out a new core curriculum; and the Wild Hope Project (see chapter 5).

ATHLETICS

In 1998 PLU left the ranks of the National Association of Intercollegiate Athletics (NAIA) and became part of the National Collegiate Athletic Association, Division III. Athletic Director Paul Hoseth said that although the NAIA had been a good fit for many years, many institutions were leaving that body and it was starting to struggle.[8] He explained that division III would be a better fit, both athletically and academically. There was some concern that it would be more difficult for many individuals to advance to national competition, but 1998-99 athletic achievements quickly ended those concerns.

PLU was represented by teams or individuals in ten national competitions during that academic year. Track and field squads had the greatest success; the men finished second and the women third at the national meets. Luke Jacobsen won the national discus championship. In fall 1998 the football team won the conference championship and reached the first round of the national playoffs. Two cross-country runners, Maree George and Ryan Pauling, were named all-Americans. The women's basketball team, led by Northwest Conference player of the year Tara Millet, advanced to the final eight of the Division III tournament. The women's softball team played in the west region tournament, and both the men's and women's tennis teams won conference crowns for retiring tennis coach Mike Benson. The men's title was the twenty-fourth in Benson's thirty years of coaching. PLU also won, for the thirteenth time in its fourteen-year history, the McIlroy-Lewis trophy, awarded to the outstanding athletic program in the Northwest Conference.

At the end of the year Hoseth predicted a bright future for the PLU athletic program, but he cautioned that the quality of the coaches was crucial. "The future is always going to depend on the quality of coaches we can attract, and not just for their sports knowledge, but for the character qualities they can bring and share with their athletes."[9]

The most dramatic athletic success of this period was the remarkable 1999 Division III national championship won by the football team. The Lutes became the first team to win the Division III title while playing every playoff game on the road. Traveling fifteen thousand miles, the team defeated Willamette University (Oregon) 28-24, Wartburg College (Iowa) 49-14, Saint John's College (Minnesota) 19-9, and Trinity University (Texas) 49-28. The championship game, the Amos Alonzo Stagg Bowl in Salem, Virginia, pitted the Lutes against heavily favored Rowan University of New Jersey. Featured on national television, the 42-13 upset is one of the greatest victories in PLU's football history. Rowan, an institution of more than seven thousand students, was playing in its fifth Stagg Bowl of the 1990s and had just snapped powerful Mount Union's fifty-four game winning streak. PLU's offensive stars were quarterback Chad Johnson, coach Frosty Westering's grandson, wide receiver Todd McDevitt, who scored two touchdowns, and running back Anthony Hicks, a two-time Northwest Conference offensive player of the year. That season Hicks shattered all the school rushing records. The defense dominated from the beginning of the game: Rowan rushed for minus sixty-three yards and had four turnovers. Capping an extraordinary season, Frosty Westering was named Division III coach of the year.

Excitement continued into the next season. In its college football 2000 issue, *Sports Illustrated* ranked PLU first in its preseason rankings (Rowan was eighth), and featured the program in an article titled, "The Nicest Team in Football." The article began with wide receiver Todd McDevitt's "epiphany" while playing for Western Washington University against the Lutes. Describing the light shining off the gold helmets of the Lutes, he said, "It was almost spiritual. Our uniforms were dark; theirs were white. We were swearing and yelling, 'Kill the Lutes!' They were helping each other off the ground, helping us off the ground. . . . They're holding hands in the huddle, praying. I thought that's what I want. Inside, I started pulling for those guys." He transferred and joined "the nicest team in America," the team with EMAL (Every Man A Lute) on their jerseys.

One of the most moving responses to the team and the fifteen thousand playoff miles traveled the previous season came from a TWA flight attendant who wrote to say how much she had enjoyed working with the team. "It's easy to see how these guys would have been a flight attendant's dream: The traveling Lutes serenaded the crew, dutifully read their passenger safety cards, looked around for the nearest exit and, over time, learned to click their 50-plus seat belts in unison."[10]

Sports Illustrated described Coach Frosty Westering as a "shambling former Marine drill instructor with kind eyes and artificial hips" who dwells on the importance of "put-ups"—the opposite of put-downs. It reported that he also inveighs against "Number 1 or No One," the attitude that if you don't finish first, you may as well not have competed. Westering encourages his players to avoid the winning-is-everything trap by competing not against their opponent but against their "best selves," becoming the best players they can be.[11]

In December 2000 it was announced that quarterback Chad Johnson had received the Gagliardi Trophy, one of two major awards given to a Division III football player. Criteria for the award included excellence in athletics, academics, and community service. Johnson was also selected to the 2000 American Football Coaches Association Good Works Team, named a Division III all-American quarterback, and selected as a Lutheran Brotherhood Lutheran College Player of the Year.[12]

At the end of the 2003 football season seventy-five year old Frosty Westering retired. His achievements were remarkable: four national championships in eight title game appearances, nineteen national postseason appearances, thirty-two consecutive winning seasons at PLU, and a 305-96-7 win-loss record in thirty-nine seasons, including a 261-70-5 record at PLU. He is one of only ten college coaches with 300 or more career wins. His inexhaustible supply of aphorisms sum up the life-lessons he valued more than victories: "The big time is not a place, but a state of heart;" "We don't have a good day, we make it a good day;" "It's not something you get, it's something you become."[13] His retirement was covered by local television stations, in a richly illustrated fourteen-page supplement in Tacoma's *News Tribune*, and a page-long article in *The Sunday Oregonian*.[14] He was succeeded as football coach by his son Scott, an all-American tight end at PLU who had been offensive coordinator since 1984.

THE YEAR 2000

Alcohol consumption and university policy once again became an issue in the fall of 1999. In an article by Kelly Kearsley, "Booze In The Hood," the *Mast* reported that parties, noise, and garbage were creating conflict in Parkland neighborhoods. Families with children were especially concerned. The same problems existed at the University of Puget Sound. Student reaction was defiant. Those contacted said they were paying rent to a landlord, not PLU, and the university couldn't regulate what went on. A columnist wrote that drinking was inevitable, but urged good judgment.[15]

In November, the *Mast* included an especially relevant special supplement, "Changing of the Guard," edited by Eric Ruthford. Under the leadership of editor Laura Ritchie, the paper was unusually well edited and written during this time. Ruthford asked what the institution would be like in the near future with large-scale retirements under way. Faculty members who had tackled the school's problems and achieved its transformations of the previous thirty years—university status, purpose, identity, governance, financial crises, community—would soon be gone. How would the large numbers of new faculty adjust to the specific culture of PLU after graduate schools' powerful emphasis on professionalism, loyalty to an academic discipline, and scholarly publication? Would new leaders emerge? How should new faculty and staff be introduced to their new setting and responsibilities?

Ruthford interviewed the provost, students, some older faculty, and half a dozen new faculty. Responses varied widely. New music faculty member and PLU graduate Svend Rønning thought "we are much less idealistic than the previous generation. I think we're much more career oriented." Another new faculty member thought that his generation had no defining political moment—like 1968—to give it identity. Contributing to the quality of university community did not resonate with some of the respondents.[16] A younger faculty meant the future would have a different texture, but the particulars were not yet clear.

Concerns about the new millennium appeared in December 1999. Such concerns were worldwide, of course, and they stretched from predictions about a fiery apocalypse to concerns about whether computer-based systems would be able to turn the millennial corner. When the *Mast* asked, "Is it the end of the world or just the start of a new year?" campus pastor Dennis Sepper answered that the world's end "could be tomorrow, and it could be another millennium away. God is in control of history."[17] The computer corner was turned and fiery apocalyptic predictions proved to be nugatory.

ISSUES AND POLITICS

In February 2000 it was announced that Eve Ensler's 1998 controversial play "The Vagina Monologues" would be presented on campus. Aiming to inform people about issues of female sexuality and to stop violence against women, the play's subjects included the first menstural period, rape, incest, domestic battery, genital mutilation, lesbianism, and self-discovery. Although perceptions of an anti-male bias continue to be debated, the *Mast's* two-page response with photos was laudatory: writers called it an "amazing, powerful play" in which "many important issues were brought out."[18] Columnist Erica Rische declared that "the typical view of female sexuality in our culture is one dimensional and this play offers multiple perspectives to a diversity of voices on female sexuality."[19] Many cast members expressed excitement and satisfaction as a result of participation. The president's office, however, received some letters critical of the performance.

On 29 April U.S. presidential candidate John McCain held a rally in Olson Auditorium before a capacity crowd; he was presented with a NCAA Division III championship t-shirt. He highlighted his reform activities and spoke of being proud that special interests opposed him. The McCain appearance and speech—obviously partisan—were possibly at odds with university policy prohibiting partisan political events on campus. President Anderson said he didn't know when the policy was written and didn't think it was violated, since there was educational benefit and no university funds were expended. ASPLU president Robby Larson said the policies needed to be clearer, and *Mast* editor Laura Ritchie admonished the president: "If President Anderson's office wants students to obey campus policy, it would do well to begin by adhering to the rules itself. There are means for changing outmoded policies. Ignoring their presence is not one of them."[20] She made it clear she was opposed not to the McCain rally but to ignoring the rules. PLU has a long tradition of welcoming politicos on campus, perhaps especially U.S. vice presidents: Hubert Humphrey in 1966, Al Gore in 1994, and Walter Mondale in 2007.

GRAFFITI

On 3 November 2000 the atmosphere in which sexual orientation was being discussed was roiled by the appearance of graffiti—"God hates fags"—painted on administration building windows overnight. President Anderson immediately wrote to the PLU community: "This past Friday offensive and shameful graffiti attacking gay and lesbian persons was painted on the Hauge administration building. Because this deplorable act violates both the core values and the policies of the university, we are aggressively seeking to identify those responsible." He asked for help in that matter and asked that everyone again commit themselves "to building a positive campus climate of inclusion, support and affirmation."[21]

Provost Paul Menzel and Vice President Laura Majovski also responded with a memorandum to faculty, staff, and administrators. They reiterated that "such expressions are blatant violations of university policies and will not be tolerated. The university policies . . . unequivocally affirm the dignity of every individual in the PLU community."[22] They described multiple opportunities for discussion in the week ahead and reported that the president would soon appoint a University Commission on Campus Climate to plan events to enhance discussion of civility and toleration issues and make recommendations. That activity was scattered over the next several months. The commission discovered problems of various sorts to be addressed.

The ten-member commission delivered its report on 13 March 2001.[23] After describing its methodology, the report stated: "PLU students, faculty and staff agree that this is a remarkable community whose potential is not yet reflected in our reality. They share a vision of a community grounded in both faith and reason, and yearn for those ideals to be lived more intentionally through stronger connections with each other and visible support for inclusion and diversity."

The commission's assessment focused on five themes related to community.

On Identity it noted that "students, faculty and staff alike are uninformed regarding the mission of PLU. Our lack of a working mission statement has affected the identity of this university. Accordingly, students, faculty and staff project their own perceptions of educational mission onto the university. PLU needs to be more intentional about developing a common understanding of purpose among all members of our community." It also pointed to affinity groups "that foster a sense of belonging but carry with them a potential for exclusion. Groups with opposing views on various issues may drown the voices of those in the middle." Means of advising student activity groups were perceived as ineffective. On Geography, the commission observed that division of students—upper and lower campus; on-campus, off-campus, and commuters—contribute to a climate of disconnection and disenfranchisement. In matters of bureaucracy, respondents felt underutilized and underappreciated. They believed that human resources are not utilized to the full advantage of the university, and sought a more friendly, inclusive, and responsive system. Of faculty, staff and student relations, participants thought that ties between these groups were inadequate. Students wanted faculty and staff to take interest in their lives, not just their formal education.

The commission's report advanced sixty recommendations organized in five groupings: articulating the university mission more effectively, creating and facilitating dialogue, improving the first-year experience program, coordinating student groups and activities, and miscellaneous. Four recommendations were thought to be crucially important: (1) revise and clarify the university mission; (2) revise the new student orientation program; (3) revise the critical conversation courses; and (4) coordinate student religious activities more deliberately and effectively. All recommendations received immediate attention.

RELIGIOUS ENTHUSIASM

The commission's description of groups that might become exclusive, and its recommendation to better coordinate religious activity, stemmed from varying expressions of religious life on campus. Much was relatively traditional, satisfying to participants and noncontroversial, but other expressions, pulsating with enthusiasm, were exclusionary and highly critical of what they lamented as an unfortunate religious status quo. Some groups had a relatively large following. In the heady atmosphere of sexual orientation discussions, "The Vagina Monologues," and the November graffiti, some of the religious groups came to the attention of the larger university community. Several had emerged in the late 1990s, led by unusually determined and organized leaders, including group worship leaders, dormitory resident assistants, well-known athletes, and two student body presidents.

When Nancy Connor and Dennis Sepper came as campus pastors in 1995 they heard from the call committee and students a clear desire for more unity among Christian groups on campus. Connor and Sepper tried to find a place for all the groups within campus ministry; they met with leaders, invited them to participate in chapel, and looked for ways to work together on campus and in service to the community. Some groups rejected this opportunity and pursued independent visions of what needed to be done. Their leaders came from student government and residential life structures where various kinds of evangelism were pushed. They organized an Eternal Victory March, inviting all Christian groups to a campus march of prayer for the salvation of students, and they sponsored a Passion Week conference with off-campus speakers. There was even an attempt to establish a university-wide orthodoxy oath. Much of this activity was at odds with PLU's ecumenical vision, but the university—and certainly residential life administrators—had been slow to respond. That began to change.

Some of the groups were variants of national organizations like Inter-Varsity Christian Fellowship and Young Life. They were aggressively evangelistic and often exclusionary. The Washington state leadership of Inter-Varsity was intensely fundamentalist during the 1990s departing from the historic English evangelical roots of the organization. Inter-Varsity controlled friendships, courting, and more. It shunned persons who left the organization.

Other groups were peculiar to Parkland and PLU. Some were supported by the fundamentalist and expansionist Clover Creek Bible Fellowship, which saw PLU as part of its mission field. One of those groups was Nu Song, a missionary-minded organization that required a public affirmation of faith and regularly dealt with issues relevant to college students like courtship, relationships, and friends; Nu Song encouraged members to practice subtle "backdoor" evangelism in public. There was considerable interest in "Exodus International North America," a group formed in 1976 that claimed to deprogram homosexuals "through the power of Jesus Christ."

The Well was a larger and popular organization, devoted to contemporary, rock-oriented worship and Bible teaching. It was connected to Clover Creek ministries, but led by students. Participants—often hundreds of them—typically met in the University Center. In addition to weekly services the Well featured retreats, Bible studies, and ten-point accountability questions to be answered each week. Participants' concerns about campus religion courses prompted a rating system: religion department faculty were graded on an acceptability scale and the grades were passed around to influence course selection. The Well was ambivalent about homosexuality; it emphasized acceptance of individuals, but sharply disapproved of the orientation and urged homosexuals to change. Some of these emphases and activities elicited satirical responses from Hinderlie Hall savants and the Daily Flyer.[24]

The Upper Room (connected to the Puget Sound Christian Center, a non-denominational Pentecostal church in Tacoma) was further afield theologically and in its worship style. Some of its leaders tried to take over the evening time slot of Rejoice—a long-time group that met for singing and worship—but when the university resisted, it acquired a separate time. Its worship style was charismatic, with speaking in tongues, and often included fiery guest speakers. There was much discussion of eschatology and harsh judgments of those whose beliefs didn't measure up. A student analysis of religion on campus reported that The Upper Room considered PLU a place "of great sin. It is their stance that one prominent member of the religion department is specifically demonized because of his affinity to Buddhism." The report noted that other PLU faculty, students, and administrators were also thought to be "courted by demons."[25] There was confidence and energy in The Upper Room, but also irresponsibility and biblical, theological, and historical ignorance of a remarkable sort.

The diverse emphases of religious life on campus became a matter of greater concern and attention as the new millennium unfolded. The report of the University Commission on Campus Climate spurred the religion department, student life office, campus ministry, and a variety of student groups to address the complicated situation. Contemporary worship styles, religious self-help, and Bible studies were not problems, but exclusionary postures and aggressive fundamentalism, anti-intellectualism, and judgmentalism were. While the latter stances appear at colleges and universities all over the United States, they had no place at a university like PLU that attempts to bring reason and faith together in an appropriate way while respecting academic freedom. Civility was crucial to that effort, but student leaders and members of Nu Song, The Well, and The Upper Room devoted almost no time and energy to understanding the nature of a Lutheran university.

Nearly all of these issues came into sharp focus in a 15 September 2000 letter in the *Mast* written by senior English major Shannon Thomas and the heated responses that flowed in throughout the fall semester. She wrote to freshmen, warning them that The Well might seem simply "a Christian group that worships together each week to make themselves feel really good about being Christians," but it was, she asserted, in fact the opposite of everything that makes for a good college experience. Its members are open to new ideas only if they fit into the "neat little box" of what they know to be true. They preach about love, she wrote, but can't practice it in real life. She cited the group's condemnation of a proposed regional "Queer Conference" on campus as evidence that "The Well openly denies the humanity of other people." She asked: "Are there members of The Well that feel differently?" She added that sexual minorities don't need The Well's prayers; if anything, they need its members to quit hiding behind Bible quotations and act like Christians, and more importantly like human beings.

She urged freshmen to be wary: "What The Well ultimately offers is hypocrisy, the status quo, and intolerance. Is that what you want out of college?"[26] The *Mast* editor appended that The Well was now called Jam 62.

Letters flowed in; many were supportive, others critical. They offered a spectrum of advice: less emotion, more civility, more careful interpretation of scripture, more literal reading of scripture, loving the individual and hating the sin, more toleration, less toleration, and so on. The nature of a university society and culture was addressed in only one letter. In response to the notion that you could love the sinner but hate the sin, Harmony advisor Beth Kraig wrote: "Think about how it would feel to have people condescendingly suggest that they 'love you' when they in fact are arguing for condemnation of the actual love that centers your existence."[27] Religion professor Samuel Torvend wrote that while it's easy to argue that personal experience, the Bible, or science has the last word, the search for truth is not that easy: "our deeply held convictions are simply not big enough to contain the mystery of who we are as sexual beings."[28]

When the vandalism—"God hates fags"—appeared in November 2000, letters to the editor lurched in that direction. They uniformly condemned that act for the rest of the semester.

Religious enthusiasm, sexual orientation, tolerance, civility, academic freedom, biblical interpretation, and the identity of a university like PLU swirled together during the 2000-2001 academic year. The university's various responses made its identity clearer. The Campus Ministry Council constitution was revised to make its Lutheran Christian nature absolutely clear; there would be no faculty and staff orthodoxy oaths. Campus pastor Dennis Sepper wrote *What's in a Middle Name? What It Means to Attend a Lutheran College or University*, which went out to all new students, and workshops on the Lutheran view of higher education became part of the training for admissions counselors, resident directors, and resident assistants. A new Diversity Center opened in 2001 with a commitment to multiculturalism and an inclusive campus. The Campus Ministry hired two senior interns to organize a range of new worship and Bible study opportunities, and in 2001 PLU graduate Sarah Wolbrecht was hired as the first full-time Peer Ministry Coordinator to work specifically with students.

Biblical interpretation, a lively issue in the fall debates, reappeared dramatically after a February 2001 lecture by the provocative New Testament scholar Marcus Borg. Author of eleven books, including the best-selling *Seeing Jesus Again for the Very First Time*, Borg was a Concordia College graduate with an Oxford D.Phil. degree. More than five hundred people packed the lecture room and hallway. He said that modern society has a "tin ear" for metaphor; many can't accept that a metaphor is not more or less true than a fact. "People have mythologized the disciples' history and literalized their myths."[29] The question and answer period was electric.

Religion professor Douglas Oakman, himself an important New Testament scholar, noted that when Borg said faith was not about "belief," he might have added that the university also is concerned not with "belief," but the critical examination of beliefs. "There are real alternatives to the false dilemmas and supposed absolutes of fundamentalism." Oakman stressed that "critical alternatives deserve to be heard and understood, not dismissed; that is at the deepest heart and mission of an excellent university education."[30] His response was apposite not only for critics of Borg's lecture, but also the critics from Nu Song, Jam 62, and The Upper Room.

TRAGEDY

Tragedy hit the PLU campus with great power twice in the winter and spring of 2001. In late February, at an off-campus party attended by as many as four hundred students, an overloaded outdoor deck collapsed, killing freshman student Monica Lightell and injuring several other students. There was alcohol at the party, but it was not involved with the collapse of the deck. Lightell had lived ten years in Panama, and she loved to talk about that experience and listen to Latin and salsa music. Friends praised her witty, vibrant personality, saying that she didn't walk into a room, she burst in. They recounted that she loved to dance and sing and would jump on a chair with a hairbrush for a microphone and perform, true to her creed that "You only live once. Life is not a dress rehearsal. Make each day count."[31] Lightell's friends called a campus memorial service on 2 March "A Celebration of Life."

On 18 May the Tacoma *News Tribune*'s inch-high headline read "PLU prof shot dead: victim is random target of stalker, who fatally shoots self." The story explained that "a man who stalked a Pacific Lutheran University music instructor for years walked onto the campus Thursday and, knowing she wasn't there, randomly selected a popular colleague of hers and shot him dead." The shooter, Donald Cowan, a fifty-five-year-old man who had briefly dated horn instructor Kathleen Farner in high school, then shot himself and died at Madigan Army Medical Center. The victim was James Dale—Jim—Holloway, a popular and gifted music instructor and the university organist. Police found a sixteen-page handwritten note detailing Cowan's plan to vent his anger at Farner (who was on sabbatical leave in Germany) by killing an innocent person. They had dated for two weeks in high school, and Cowan was obsessed that the brief romance had ended without a good bye hug. Cowan's 1995 attempt to rekindle the brief relationship resulted in an anti-harassment order.

"Almighty Lord, we find ourselves in this place again," university pastor Dennis Sepper said at a gathering an hour after the shooting. "Give us the courage and strength to face the next hours, which will be difficult."

Jim Holloway was born in Georgia and educated there (Shorter College) and in Texas (The University of North Texas). A long-time pastoral musician, he served parishes in Georgia, Texas, Alabama, and Oregon as organist and choir director before moving to Tacoma in 1989 to become Minister through Music at Parkland's Trinity Lutheran Church. While at Trinity he established one of the largest and most active church music programs in the Northwest while teaching part-time at PLU. After finishing his doctorate at the University of Washington he joined the music faculty and became the university organist. He was a remarkably gifted and prize-winning musician, a teacher and friend, a gourmet cook, and a teller of—sometimes outrageous—jokes. His death was a terrible loss to his family, to PLU, and to the world of music.

President Loren Anderson pointed out in an 18 May chapel service, the day after the shooting, that Holloway was not only a gifted musician but a poet whose "gift for verbal expression was rare and priceless. And like his music, Jim spoke from the heart!—with a depth and richness and delight that transformed routine conversation into intellectual adventure." The president noted that Holloway's chapel homily on 25 February, shortly after the death of Monica Lightell, reflected both his depth of feeling and his power with language. He had spoken that day of the journey of the Magi:

> We in the university must bring our gifts: scholarship and faith, questions and vision, disagreements and dialogue, confusion and wonderment, patience and humility. The gifts have a place at the foot of the crèche and in the shadow of the cross. As God did not reject their curious gifts, may we too pray that the learned, the delicate, the forgotten and those who died young shall not be forgotten at the throne of God, when the simple come into their kingdom.

Holloway's memorial service—"A Celebration of the Life of James Dale Holloway"—was filled with music, including two pieces he had written: "Love is His Name," and "Suffering Savior," a jazz canticle. The University Symphony played and the Choir of the West sang, as did the crowd that filled Eastvold Auditorium to overflowing. Bishop David Wold gave the homily.

ROTC

Since 1985 PLU had allowed ROTC (Reserve Officers' Training Corps) training on its campus, with Seattle University as the Host Battalion and PLU as a "cross-enrolled" school. That meant PLU reported to the professor of military science at Seattle University, who completely controlled the PLU program. Small in the 1980s, in the 1990s it grew much larger and soon became more active and successful than the program at the host institution. In 2001 the Department of the Army invited PLU to become an autonomous Host Battalion program; the offer to move in this way was unprecedented. PLU would gain new and enhanced scholarships if the transition took place, as well as more male and ethnically diverse students, more equipment, and a larger budget. What would happen if the proposal was rejected was not clear. The present arrangement might simply continue, or the ROTC program at PLU might be eliminated. In its long-range budget planning the army assumed the offer would be accepted.

Various concerns quickly emerged. What would be the academic rank and status of the professor of military science? How would the program be represented on the appropriate academic committees, and what supervision and control would the university have over the program? The administration and Educational Policies Committee promptly determined that the president and provost would decide on rank, the provost would be the program representative, and the professor of military science would have the same responsibilities and standards of conduct as other members of the faculty. The provost consulted five institutions, one Lutheran and four Roman Catholic, to assess their experiences with ROTC. Their responses were positive.[32]

The heated concern that emerged from some faculty and students was not about ROTC training or a possible administrative shift from Seattle to Tacoma, but about the army's 1993 "Don't Ask, Don't Tell, Don't Pursue, Don't Harass" policy (it added "harass" in 1997). Was that policy at odds with the university's non-discrimination policy? If so, how should the discrepancy be resolved? The ROTC program on campus predated the non-discrimination policy. The provost's office distributed a helpful thirty-two-page "voters guide," a collection of information and opinion pieces, to assist faculty in decision making. The guide ended with this advice:

> Approval of this proposal will allow PLU to attain academic autonomy, increase assets provided by the D A in manpower and equipment, increased efficiency in the administrative processing of cadets, and will allow the institution to receive recognition nationally for its outstanding ROTC program. The effect on training our nation's future leaders, both militarily and civilian, to lead lives of service in an ethical and moral manner, can only be enhanced by approval of this action.[33]

The faculty vote at its 20 April meeting was preceded by a debate about who could vote, lively student-faculty discussions, and petitions (over nine days without a signature venue, students against the ROTC proposal had gathered 136 signatures; in four days with a signature table in the front of the University Center, students in support of the proposal had gathered 771 signatures). The afternoon of the faculty meeting fifty students opposed to the proposal stood outside Ler-

aas Lecture Hall in silent protest. Faculty chair Norris Peterson allowed one hour
for debate. It was wide-ranging, but increasingly it became a plebiscite on the
army's "Don't Ask, Don't Tell" policy. That the ROTC program—still administered at Seattle University—would continue even with a no vote was rarely men-
tioned by those who opposed the proposal. Forceful support came from members
of the school of nursing. The offer to become a host institution was accepted, 80-
62.[34] Letters to the *Mast* about the matter continued the rest of the spring. After
a long discussion the board of regents approved the expansion at its May 2001
meeting. Board chair Gary Severson said it would be a "positive opportunity for
both the army and PLU."[35]

Ten Years Later

The first ten years of Loren Anderson's presidency flew by rapidly. The major
challenges of enrollment and finance were brought under control, though not de-
finitively solved. Only a major increase in endowment income would accomplish that. There were advances, however, and growing the endowment remained
a major item on the development agenda. Buildings were built. In addition to
the Mary Baker Russell Music Center—a wonderful gift to music faculty, students, the university, and the community—in late 1999 the Keck Observatory
was dedicated. The result of a $500,000 gift from the W. W. Keck Foundation,
it featured a sixteen-inch Schmidt-Cassegrain reflecting telescope and five smaller
eight-inch telescopes. It was located on lower campus, surrounded by playing
fields. The grant also provided for a mapping center that included a global po-
sitioning system, a research grade seismometer, a weather station, and environmental monitoring equipment. The program would focus on observing known
asteroids and searching for unknown ones. Physics professor Steve Starkovich
was the project coordinator.

The refurbishing of Xavier Hall, completed in 2001, brought an up-to-date
infrastructure into one of the most interesting buildings on campus. The most
appealing and important features of the old building were preserved, but func-
tionally it was brought into the 21st century. The original light-filled library reading room, turned into a lecture hall in 1967, was restored. South Hall, an
imaginative, multi-faceted dormitory with variously shaped and sized rooms designed for upper-class and married students, opened in 2000. It proved very
popular and brought some students back to campus who would otherwise have
chosen to live in apartments.

There were also significant achievements in the operation and direction of
the university. *PLU 2000*'s axioms guided institutional decisions over the next
decade, and the reform in faculty governance proved beneficial. Faculty scholarship jumped several notches. For example, in 2002 the Humanities Division

took comprehensive stock of current faculty's scholarly achievements. The inventory included thirty published books, forty edited or co-edited books, eleven edited collections, six translations and critical editions, over three hundred peer-reviewed articles, and one hundred twenty book reviews. Other branches of the university were equally productive. Sexual orientation was discussed openly and, for the most part, with civility. When not, the problems were quickly addressed. ANAC membership appears to have helped the university focus more sharply when questions of purpose and identity arose; such summary descriptions in *PLU 2000* and *PLU 2010* are important evidence testifying to greater clarity and confidence.

In addition to enrollment, financial, and fundraising issues, the most significant challenge facing the university as the new millennium began was the changing complexion and identity of its faculty and staff. In the aftermath of widespread retirements, would the best and most important features of the institution's culture and tradition survive (community, participatory governance, searches for meaning, commitment to teaching, centrality of the faith-reason dialectic, and academic freedom)? What would new faculty, staff, and administrators do with that culture and tradition? How would it be adapted? Would leaders emerge? Questions of that sort were raised in a provocative lecture entitled "The Vocation of a Christian University in a Globalized World," delivered at PLU in the spring of 2002 by the University of California, Berkeley, scholar Robert Bellah. It bears reading and re-reading. He described the scholar's vocation as standing for something.

> And the metaphor of standing for something implies also the metaphor of a ground on which to stand. What is the ground on which the scholar and the university must stand? One might say values, but I have chosen another term: again provisionally, I will say that the ground is meaning, and here I want deliberately to distinguish meaning from information.[36]

He explained how tradition helps find that meaning and why the constant examination and re-examination of tradition are necessary for an appropriately lived life and a healthy university: "we are by nature creatures of tradition because we do not make up the world in which we live but must come to terms with what is given to us which is almost everything."[37] Following Jaroslav Pelikan, he distinguished between traditionalism—the dead faith of the living, a mindless repetition of the past—and tradition, the living faith of the dead.[38] Can tradition and meaning, understood in this way, be relevant for a generation of faculty members schooled in professionalism, with loyalty to disciplines and scholarly publication more than to institutional communities? How will the neuralgic problems of modernism and post-modernism be addressed as the next genera-

100 Distinguished Alumni, 1990

President William Rieke with Namibian students

PLU presidents Loren Anderson and William Rieke

NAIA National Championship softball team

Lagerquist Concert Hall, including the Gottfried and Mary Fuchs Organ

MaryAnn, Loren and Maren Anderson, 1992

Vice President William Frame

Economics Professor Stanley Brue

Physics Professor K.T. Tang

Philosophy Professor and Provost
Paul Menzel

History Professor Beth Kraig

English Professor Tom Campbell

History Professor Chris Browning

Queen Sonja and King Harald of Norway with the Andersons, 1995

Chemistry Professor and
Vice President Sheri Tonn

Vice President
Laura Majovski

Religion Professor and
Provost Patricia
O'Connell Killen

1999 Football Team with Washington Governor Gary Locke

Music Professor Jim Holloway

Wang Center Founders Peter and Grace Wang

"China: Bridges for a New Century," Wang Center Symposium, 2003

Regent Don Morken and Wanda Morken

Garfield Book Company at PLU, 2007

Choir of the West Director Richard Nance

KPLU General Manager Martin Neeb

University Commons, remodeled in 2007

Parkland Elementary School – East Campus

Mary Baker Russell Music Center

Mary Baker Russell Music Center and Chihuly Glass Sculptures

Mary Baker Russell Music Center Organ Installation by Paul Fritts

Keck Observatory

South Hall

Morken Center for Learning and Technology

Morken Center for Learning and Technology

Morken Center for Learning and Technology

Garfield Commons, including the Garfield Book Company at PLU

Garfield Commons, including the Garfield Book Company at PLU

tion seeks meaning? Bellah argued that "modernity has given us instruments, material and cultural, of great power but it has not shown us what to do with them."[39] Surely the reappropriation and use of tradition to help discover meaning and direction in a world where the map has been lost, is a task that universities—and certainly PLU—need to embrace. How a new and younger faculty will do that will be the most interesting chapter in the next history of Pacific Lutheran University.

President Anderson was both realistic and optimistic about the university's future in an interview in the fall 2002 *Scene*: "10 Years and Still Focused on the Future." He said the biggest fundraising challenge the university faced was the "revitalization of the schoolhouse;" maintaining and renovating buildings built in the 1950s and 1960s was especially important. Eastvold and several dormitories needed refurbishing, and funding for the Morken Center for Learning and Technology was not completed. Discussing the problems of the early 1990s and the reform in faculty governance, he stressed "the importance of candor in addressing the challenges and problems we face. The past 10 years have been a real time of learning for me. I'm a much, much stronger proponent of democracy than I was 10 years ago." He emphasized the need to trust the strengths of the institution and its people, and to work together as a community. "So, we now have a governance system that spins and sputters and sometimes doesn't always move very fast, but when the day is over, it acquits itself very well." He thought the prospects for Lutheran higher education had never been brighter: "Today, more than ever, our convictions that life is a gift from God, that life has a purpose, that the human experience is transcendent, and that we are ultimately created to be a positive force in the world resonates with people from all faith backgrounds, as well as those who come out of no faith background at all."[40]

CHAPTER FIVE

INTERNATIONALIZING THE INSTITUTION

Chapter Five

INTERNATIONALIZING THE INSTITUTION

PACIFIC LUTHERAN UNIVERSITY has always attempted to match its ecumenical educational vision with its curriculum and activities. For example, the 1903-04 liberal arts and teacher training curricula included the histories of Greece, Rome, the Middle Ages, modern Europe, England, and the United States; English literature, Greek, Latin, German, and Norwegian were also required. There was much campus interest in the Middle East, China, and Japan as well, and one of the earliest faculty members was soon a missionary in China. Concerns stretching beyond the Pacific Northwest continued through the 1920s and 1930s, culminating with the creation of the Pacific Historical Society of the Baltic Peoples. Its collections would center not only on the Norwegian Americans who founded PLU, but on all the Baltic peoples. Publications would follow so that the considerable influence exerted in both Europe and on the Pacific coast would be understood. "Those who have a rich historical past have a more abundant future," the society's founders wrote.[1] Research and archival work would center in the new library, whose ground breaking took place in April 1937. The ambitions of the society's founders were thwarted by the pressures of World War II, but they reflected an educational philosophy that continues to shape the institution.

During the 1940s and 1950s the college emphasized finding jobs and in the 1950s student apathy about politics, world affairs, and contemporary intellectual development was widespread. A few PLU students began to study abroad, however, and 1953 alumnus Lloyd Eastman, the first PLU graduate to acquire a Ph.D. in history (from Harvard), was thought to be the world's foremost expert on Chiang Kai-Shek and the Kuomintong era in China when he came to PLU in 1986 to deliver the Schnackenberg Lecture.[2] Despite the passivity of the 1950s, intellectual life flourished in spots with exciting results. Student activism and intellectual life advanced mightily during the 1960s and a global vision accompanied both. The climax was the first annual West Coast China Conference, organized and directed by students, held in February 1968. A number of internationally known scholars participated.[3]

By the end of the 1970s the curriculum was significantly internationalized, foreign study had grown dramatically, and the number of international students continued to increase. In 1978 a Foreign Area Studies program was organized under the whirlwind leadership of history professor Mordechai Rozanski and he was appointed director of the new Office of International Education. The new Foreign Area Studies program made PLU a "showcase institution" in the handling of global studies, according to the U.S. Office of Education.[4] Between 1978 and 1982 more than half a million dollars poured into the institution to subsidize international programs. By 1982 an interdisciplinary global studies major was also approved (it had to be a second major, complementing a disciplinary major). The program was complicated, but it allowed a relatively small institution to address the complexity of global issues in ways that single departments could not manage.[5]

Also in 1982, business professor Thad Barnowe taught management and organizational practice at China's Zhongstan University on a Fulbright grant. He was the first Fulbright lecturer in business to teach in China since 1949, and the first foreign professor to teach a subject other than languages at Zhongstan since the Cultural Revolution. Exchange programs for students and faculty were arranged with Zhongstan and Chengdu University of Science and Technology, and in 1986 sixteen students, along with chemistry professors Charles Anderson and William Giddings, went to Chengdu. That relationship still exists.[6]

Even with all these accomplishments program growth was limited in the 1980s. Programmatic approval had to trickle down through various administrative offices, and enthusiasm for new developments and administrative arrangements was sometimes muted. In addition, study abroad programs were inhibited by full tuition charges and arguments about how administrative costs should be allocated. Political science professor Ann Kelleher led the battle against these problems and she spearheaded much of the programmatic advance after Rozanski's movement into university administration. (He has most recently been president of Guelf University in Canada and Rider University in New Jersey).

Most of these administrative and financial problems were resolved with the coming of Loren Anderson as president in 1992 and his understanding that international education should be a fundamental feature of PLU. Kelleher said, "Things took off in the mid-90s with both bottom-up activity and top-down support."[7] Advances included departmental curricular and co-curricular developments, greater emphasis on J-Term courses, the Trinidad semester, a Center for International Programs, a new language laboratory, an international student admissions director, and a number of foundation and government grants. In addition to Kelleher, those most heavily involved in advancing international education in the '90s were Roberta Brown, Judy Carr, Barbara Temple-Thurston, Audun Toven, and Tamara Williams.

THE WANG CENTER

International education got a substantial boost with the 7 December 2001 announcement that a four million dollar gift from 1960 graduate Peter Wang and his wife Grace would fund the development of an international education center at PLU, soon named The Wang Center for International Programs. The events of 11 September 2001 motivated the gift. Wang, a native of Taiwan, was a mathematics and physics major at PLU who earned a Ph.D. in probability theory at Wayne State University; Grace received a Ph.D. in chemistry from the same institution. After teaching mathematics and statistics at several universities, in 1970 Wang began a fourteen-year teaching career in mathematics and national security affairs at the Naval Post Graduate School in Monterey, California. Wang is considered one of the nation's top researchers in the use of mathematical models and probability theories for predicting and assessing security threats.[8] In 1986 he left teaching to establish several international trade ventures, develop computer assisted engineering data handling systems, and, with his wife, manage the family's highly successful real estate acquisition and management interests. But, according to Wang, making money isn't everything. "One of the things that Grace and I decided early on was to live our lives in the style of a college professor. Living modestly, you can only spend so much money. That enables you to use your wealth to make a difference in the world. That is how we were able to establish the Wang Center and realize our dream."[9] The center emphasized: (1) strengthening current programs, (2) expanding faculty and student research, and (3) providing public education through regular symposiums and forums.

In fall 2002 Janet Rasmussen, a former faculty member, was named interim director of the Wang Center. After leaving PLU she had served as dean at Nebraska Wesleyan and president of Hollins University in Roanoke, Virginia.

The first Wang Center symposium—"China: Bridges for a New Century"— drew seven hundred people from the Asian, business, academic and PLU communities. "This symposium symbolizes our commitment to educate global citizens and peace builders, and to offer PLU to this community and region as a place where global issues are studied and discussed," President Loren Anderson said.[10] Peter Wang was overwhelmed by the response to the symposium, describing it as "the most gratifying experience of my life."[11] Featured speakers included Ambassador Wang Yunxiang from the Peoples Republic of China; John Holden, president of the National Committee on U.S.-China Relations; and Sidney Rittenberg, PLU's longtime visiting professor of Chinese studies, who was honored with the Wang Center's first Peace Builder Award for his nearly six decades of work to establish closer relations between China and the U.S. Scholars from the United States, Norway, and China, business leaders, and attorneys conducted large group sessions on China and the global economy, human rights, youth culture, school reform, and China and the U.S. in the American century. In addition, there were eight sessions on business, four on culture and the arts, and one each on health care and higher education. Wang Center grants to faculty and students were also announced. The symposium was packed with activity and people, setting a high standard for future events.

The second Wang Center Symposium—"Pathways to Peace"—was held in January 2005. It focused on the Norwegian approach to democracy and development; it also recognized the centennial celebration of Norway's separation from Sweden. Symposium topics included security, environment, human rights, and global health. More than a thousand people attended. During the opening session Norwegian ambassador to the United States Knut Vollebaek quipped: "The whole Norwegian diplomatic corps is here—don't keep us too long."[12] Norway's forty-year peacekeeping involvement in the Sudan was a featured topic, and Tom Vraalsen, Norway's special envoy to Sudan, described the bloody civil war and peace efforts going on there. It was striking that representatives from both sides of the struggle were present—the Rev. Canon Clement Janda and Salah Ahmed El Guneid, minister of the Republic of Sudan to the United States—just days after the 9 January signing of an historic peace agreement. Norway's skill-building activity in Namibia was also described and discussed at the symposium. Wang Center Peace Builder Awards were given to Tom Vraalsen, polar explorers Liv Arneson and Ann Bancroft, and the Namibia Association of Norway.

STUDY ON SEVEN CONTINENTS

The longtime enthusiasm for global studies, the emphasis on international education in long-range planning documents, and recent programmatic growth reached a dramatic climax in the 2006 J-Term when PLU students were found on all seven continents: more than three hundred students were studying in seventeen countries. Six of the groups prepared blogs about their experiences. Among the course topics were human rights and development in Namibia, the church and courts in South Africa, the natural history and the environment of Antarctica, art and music in China, children's literature in New Zealand, international media in Australia, moral philosophy in western Europe, cultural and environmental history of the Andes, and Makah culture on the Olympic Peninsula in Washington state. Newly appointed director of the Wang Center Neal Sobania said: "We refer to ourselves as a globally focused university and that is really the heart and soul of what PLU is about."[13] Mary M. Dwyer, president of the Institute for the International Education of Students and commissioner of the Abraham Lincoln Congressional Commission on Study Abroad noted:

In 2006, the U.S. Senate-designated Year of Study Abroad, it is fitting and
trailblazing for Pacific Lutheran University to be offering January term pro-
gramming on all seven continents. This is a first in the field of education abroad
and bodes well for PLU reaching its target of 50 percent of its graduating sen-
iors studying abroad by 2010. PLU's commitment to education abroad puts PLU
in the forefront of undergraduate education, where education abroad is no longer
a frill but rather central to a high quality college education.[14]

The PLU faculty's tradition of global scholarship burgeoned in the new millennium. Business professor Bill Yager taught in Nicaragua in 2002-03; communication professor Ed Inch worked on conflict resolution in Serbia and
Macedonia in 2004; that same year economics professor Priscilla St. Clair presented a paper in Ethiopia on environmental sustainability, assisted by 2004
graduate Erin Burgess, the only undergraduate to address the conference. History professor Robert Ericksen delivered papers in Germany and Poland, as did
his colleague E. Wayne Carp in England and Sweden. English professor Charles
Bergman was a Fulbright Senior Scholar in Ecuador at the Universidad San
Francisco de Quito in fall 2006. Spanish professor Tamara Williams participated in a seminar in Argentina. Anthropology professor Gregory Guldin has
published extensively about China; as an indigenous peoples specialist and a
cross-cultural consultant, he has worked on projects in China, India, Indone-
sia, the Philippines, Russia, the United States, and Vietnam for the Asian Development Bank, the European Bank for Reconstruction and Development,
and the World Bank. In April 2007 his colleague Elizabeth Brusco gave the
"Lucy Farrow" lecture at Uppsala University in Sweden and later lectured in
Stockholm on the global growth of pentecostalism.

On 22 April 2007 four composers from Sichuan Conservatory of Music in
Chengdu, China, arrived for a five-day visit with the music composition faculty
at PLU, which culminated in a concert of new Chinese and American music.
The visit complemented a trip the PLU composition faculty made to Chengdu
in March. The PLU sessions were intense as the composers learned from each
other and prepared for the concert. Music department chair David Robbins
called it "an incredible experience. It was fascinating to see how common our
musical language is—we're exploring the same international contemporary musical language."[15] Student and faculty exchanges with Sichuan had been going
on for twenty-one years, but this was the first musical exchange. Music professor Greg Youtz was the primary organizer of the event. Since visiting China on
a sabbatical leave in 1991, he has continued to share his enthusiasm for Chinese culture and music and to fuse western and eastern techniques in his own
compositions. He told Tacoma's *News Tribune* that "music perception, at some
level, is universal—people's brains all work the same way."[16]

Namibia

In February 2003 it was announced that PLU and its School of Education would help the Namibian educational system address a number of challenges. After Namibia's independence in 1990, it was working to raise its 38 percent literacy rate; it was also trying to modify its education curriculum, based on dated European models, to include concerns about democracy and social justice. PLU professors would work alongside counterparts from Hedmark University College in Norway and the University of Namibia. Five one-week workshops were planned over the next year and a half to upgrade the skills and knowledge of primary school teachers in rural Namibia. A U.S. Agency for International Development grant of a hundred thousand dollars made the cooperation possible. J-Term and semester-long courses for PLU students in Norway and Namibia resulted from this activity. Ann Kelleher, project director for the grant, said such development work was new for PLU and that PLU was the first American university to study international development issues from the Scandinavian point of view.[17]

Education professor Sue Yerian said it was thrilling to help build an educational system in the infancy of Namibia's independence as a nation. Other faculty members involved were Paula Leitz, Jan Lewis, and Louette McGraw.[18]

Fundraising and Planning

The most successful fundraising campaign in PLU's history, "The Campaign for Pacific Lutheran University: The Next Bold Step," was concluded on 31 May 2004. It raised $128.5 million in gifts, pledges, and documented deferred commitments, 30 percent more than the initial goal of $100 million. The goals of the campaign were threefold: building the endowment, strengthening annual support, and enhancing university facilities. All were met. The campaign was launched just one year after the conclusion of the $72.3 million "Make a Lasting Difference" campaign. Highlights from the campaign included: gifts from 22,000 donors; the three largest gifts of $12, $8, and $4 million came from alumni; 184 donors made gifts and pledges of $100,000 or more; the board of regents committed more than $40 million; and faculty and staff contributed more than $5 million. President Anderson's efforts to build a generous board had paid dividends.

The campaign's success fully funded the Morken Center for Learning and Technology, established the Wang Center, created ninety-seven new endowed scholarships, increased the university's endowment from $30.7 million to more than $51 million, and enabled various grants to help build programmatic activity. The campaign reinforced the university's mission and core values, according to President Loren Anderson. As one of the generous alumni, 1955 nursing graduate and regent Karen Hille Phillips, explained: "I feel strongly about educating students for lives of service in a meaningful manner. And that is our mission after all. There are many problems in the world today and we so desperately need good people to help make the world a better place. There have to be solutions found to these problems other than war—solutions through peace."[19]

The second long-range plan produced during Loren Anderson's tenure as president was called *PLU 2010: The Next Level of Distinction.* Published in January 2003, it was more broadly gauged than the earlier *PLU 2000* with its specific responses to the enrollment and financial problems of the early 1990s. Preparation for the second plan began in 1999-2000 with twenty-four "town meetings" in which more than thirteen hundred alumni and friends gathered to discuss the university's future. Consistent themes emerged from those conversations: the importance of the Lutheran heritage, the centrality of the liberal arts, the focus on global perspectives, and the emphasis on educating for lives of service. Those themes shaped the more than two years of conversations that informed the final document. The foreword to that document reaffirmed "PLU's core identity as liberal arts Lutheran university in the Pacific Northwest. That identity is the platform from which we will address the challenges of the future."[20]

The document's five chapters described identity and laid out a framework for planning and action. Each chapter concluded with a series of recommendations that needed attention, opened possibilities, and required decisions.

Chapter one was about mission. It described PLU's foundational heritage and its emphasis on intellectual freedom, vocation, and Luther's dialectical theology.

> With a daring enthusiasm for learning and a sense of vocation and service, PLU is dedicated to the highest ideals of liberal and professional education and service to others. Lutherans establish and maintain colleges and universities for these reasons—giving society the kinds of leaders and citizens it needs, the kinds who serve all of the world and work for human dignity and justice.[21]

The statement also described the importance and influence of PLU's Pacific Northwest and Pacific Rim location. Chapter one spelled out five action-oriented aspirations: cultivating academic excellence, building an engaged community, enhancing global perspectives, nurturing a sense of life as vocation, and seeking fiscal strength.

Chapter two discussed how to attract and retain students who desire the distinctive education PLU offers. It contended that the university must articulate its mission in a more clear and compelling way and ensure that recruiting and admissions processes were informed and effective. It recommended that co-curricular programs be strengthened and meshed more seamlessly with academic programs. Chapter three emphasized the need to sustain a vigorous and distinctive life of the mind and how the institution's religious and cultural identity needed to guide students as they worked out the dimensions of meaningful life and work. It also argued that "an elite education for all"—an education of the highest quality that welcomes and serves all who desire it—should be fundamental at PLU.

Chapter four spoke to the very heart of *PLU 2010*. It highlighted three areas of activity that needed greater emphasis in the next few years: person-focused holistic learning, international education, and student research and creative projects. "These three claims to distinction serve as both institutional characteristics and ideals—to a great extent they mark who we currently are, but they also powerfully inspire and boldly challenge us to become a more distinctive university."[22] Chapter five discussed aligning resources with mission, goals, and priorities.

University efforts to reach the goals and priorities were encouraged and regularly evaluated—as they had been with *PLU 2000*—by the president's, provost's and other administrative offices and by faculty committees.

THE MORKEN CENTER

By the last decade of the twentieth century the School of Business had long outgrown its administration building location and classrooms were technologically inadequate. On lower campus, financial constraints during the building of the Rieke Science Center had reduced original plans for office space, leaving mathematics, computer science, and computer engineering faculty housed in temporary quarters last expanded in 1984. Provost Paul Menzel saw important links between the three academic units, especially a need for appropriate technology and the centrality of quantitative reasoning, that could be strengthened with geographic proximity and the conversations that would more easily emerge if all were in the same building. The 1997 campus master plan included a center for learning and technology that would house all three. Funding for its construction was part of "The Campaign for Pacific Lutheran University: The Next Bold Step."

The impetus for discovering the necessary funding came from regent Don Morken, a 1960 graduate, and his wife, Wanda. He had chaired the "Make A Lasting Difference" campaign. The Morkens stepped forward with gifts totaling $8 million to launch the enterprise. Morken said timing was important; with the stock market down, it was important to act and encourage others to do the same. The gift gave him an opportunity to demonstrate his dedication to the university. He did not want the building named after himself, but President Loren Anderson insisted. Morken conceded: "if you want to put the Morken name on it, it's not just me, it's the Morken family."[23] His father, Ed, was a PLU regent for sixteen years; his mother, Cletus, was an enthusiastic supporter; his aunt, R. Eline Kraabel Morken, was director of the department of nursing from 1953 to 1966; his brother Ed and sister Betty Sue were graduates, as were his daughter Sonya (MBA) and son-in-law Tony Prata. In addition, "a whole bunch of relatives," cousins, nieces, and nephews had attended PLU.[24] Morken said he was honored to have the family name attached to the building. Funding was completed with hundreds of gifts from individuals, couples, corporations, and foundations. Plaques in rooms, wings, and plazas identify many of them.

The Morken Center for Learning and Technology took thirteen months to build and cost $21 million; it was designed by the Zimmer Gunsul Frasca Partnership architectural firm and built by Sellen Construction. The project manager was Lorig and Associates. A technological marvel, the building is packed with advanced interactive computing and multimedia resources. It is also a model of sustainability with state-of-the-art conservation and low-impact environmental features. It was built to meet the U.S. Green Building Council's guidelines for certification under the Leadership in Energy and Environmental Design, the first LEED building in Pierce County to attain the program's gold-level status. Sustainability features included concrete flooring in 65 percent of the building to reduce the use of chemical maintenance products; organic low-odor paint and glue materials; low energy glass; wheat board; a geothermal system of wells and pumps to heat and cool the building; lights in each room controlled by motion sensors to shut off when the room is empty; bamboo, a rapidly growing renewable hardwood, in the main stairway atrium; framing using 95 percent recycled steel. Ninety-three percent of the construction waste was recycled. The Morken Center is the most earth-friendly (and student-friendly) building on campus; it set new standards for all future construction and refurbishing.

Leadership for this green achievement came from many quarters. President Anderson said: "Quite frankly, we would have had a hard time reconciling any other way of building with our principles. When it can be done—and I'm here to say it can be done efficiently and cost-effectively—it should be done."[25] Yancy Wright, the Sellen Construction Company project engineer, described work on the Morken Center as a "unique case" of committed individuals working together to realize an ambitious goal. "Starting at the top with Sheri Tonn all the way through with Dave Kohler (director of Facilities Management) and Grounds Maintenance Specialist Ken Cote, . . . if it weren't for those people it wouldn't have happened."[26]

The building was dedicated on 5 May 2005. Robert B. Reich, Professor of Public Policy at the Goldman School of Public Policy at the University of California, Berkeley, and the Secretary of Labor under President Bill Clinton, spoke on "The Truth about Globalization."

Campus and community revitalization advanced significantly in the spring and summer of 2007 with the completion of the Garfield Commons and two large projects, refurbishing the University Center and Tingelstad Hall. When the University Center, built in 1970, was shut down after spring break for a major facelift, services located there, including dining service, were relocated all over campus. The Sellen Construction Company worked double shifts to complete the project by the end of August. The transformation was striking. Highrise Tingelstad Hall, built in 1967, saw a complete refurbishing. It was retrofitted to deal with earthquakes; a sprinkler system was installed; and plumbing, wiring, carpeting, bathrooms, and windows were all updated or replaced. One group of workers tackled projects from the bottom up while another group worked from the top down. Financing for both projects came from a bond issue.

The Garfield Commons, a 32,670 square-foot building on the corner of Garfield Street and Pacific Avenue, once occupied by the Piggly Wiggly grocery store and Johnson's Drug Store, anchored a community revitalization project called the Garfield Street Activity Center Plan. Participants included representatives from county government, Pierce Transit, the state Department of Transportation, Garfield businesses, the local chamber of commerce, and PLU.[27] The intent was to create a lively urban village on Parkland's main street and a more attractive entrance to the businesses located there and to the university. The Garfield Commons is the centerpiece. It houses a much-enlarged PLU bookstore (the Garfield Book Company at PLU), with rooms for community meetings, an adjoining coffee shop, Farrelli's Gourmet Wood Fire Pizza, and several additional restaurants and businesses. The eight-million-dollar project was built in partnership with Lorig and Associates, who also advised and assisted in building both the Morken Center and South Hall. The Garfield Commons opened in late July 2007 and was dedicated on 4 September.

PLU has been working for more than twenty years to create a more sustainable campus. In addition to the construction projects described above, another important example of this commitment was President Anderson's signing of the Talloires Declaration on Earth Day 2004, making PLU the first university in the Pacific Northwest to commit to incorporating sustainability and environmental literacy into all aspects of the university.[28] In 2007 Anderson joined with a dozen other college and university presidents to sign the American College and University Presidents Climate Commitment. The pledge requires universities to develop a plan to reduce greenhouse gas emissions and become carbon neutral. The effort is modeled after the U.S. Mayors Climate Protection Agreement, led by Seattle mayor Greg Nickels.

CAMPUS LIFE

Two large and important grants were received in 2002. In May PLU announced a $456,300 grant from the Teagle Foundation to strengthen and increase the visibility of international programs. Its faculty director, Spanish professor

Tamara Williams, said the funds would be used to strengthen and integrate programs that already existed and to help the institution reach its goal of distinction in international education. Those efforts would involve the entire university.

In December a $2.5 million grant from the Lilly Foundation to explore vocation was announced. Vocation had been important to PLU's understanding of its educational mission since the 1890s, and it was central to the mission statement efforts of the early 1990s. The grant, one of only forty awarded nationally, would help address that emphasis even more intentionally. The Lilly Foundation, based in Indianapolis, Indiana, supports religious, educational, and community development projects, mostly in Indiana. The application was prepared by philosophy professor and former provost Paul Menzel and religion professor Patricia Killen.

The core of the enterprise was the five-year "Wild Hope" project, which asked the central question: "What will you do with your one wild and precious life?" The project was designed by Menzel, Killen, and a committee of eight faculty and staff. They wanted it to be "organic" to PLU and to help students find their calling and purpose in life. Menzel explained: "We think college is the time to ask the big questions. What will you live for? What are you called to be and to do? How will you make a genuine contribution to the world? What is your purpose, your passion, your unique talent? At PLU we help you recognize your connection with the world and your responsibility to serve it."[29] Students also played a major role in planning activities. The completed plan included conferences, guest speakers, weekend retreats, redesigned inquiry seminars during J-Term, and faculty initiatives. About half of all freshmen participated in off-campus J-Term retreats during the five-year period. Menzel observed that the students needed only minimal guidance as they helped plan: "We were amazed at how they thought ahead of us."[30] Willie Painter, the 2005-06 ASPLU president, said that "Wild Hope teaches students a language of asking these deep, heart-wrenching, mind-boggling questions. But beyond PLU's borders, it's usually a foreign language."[31]

The university is determined to keep the program alive beyond the five-year grant; a $500,000 "sustainability" grant from Lilly will take "Wild Hope" through 2011, and efforts are under way to keep it going after that. According to Menzel continuation is crucially important: "PLU is both a contemporary institution and an institution of the church, and when you put that together you have a group of people who have an obligation to look at this."[32]

ADMINISTRATIVE FLUX

Alongside the remarkable achievements and advances of the first part of the twenty-first century—financial, demographic, academic, architectural, environmental—was a considerable amount of administrative instability. As the level of institutional achievement rose, so did expectations placed on both faculty and administration. Meanwhile, the pool of outstanding and experienced candidates for administrative positions sometimes seemed very small. Candidates were hard to find. Length of administrative service throughout the country, and certainly at PLU, was often brief.

In 2002 a new provost, James Pence, was appointed to replace Paul Menzel after his eight years of estimable service. A Colorado State University graduate with a Ph.D. degree in English from the University of Arizona, Pence had served as associate vice president at Southern Colorado University, as vice president for Academic Affairs and dean at Wartburg College, and most recently as provost and dean of the Faculty at St. Olaf College. He declared that his own frequent career moves had given him great respect for the challenges newcomers often face.[33] It was hoped his years of experience would mesh effectively with the multiple activities and various needs at PLU. Making academic administration more efficient and streamlined, a possible new core curriculum, international education, and a dramatic influx of new and younger faculty were all paramount concerns.

Pence's tenure did not go well, however. The new provost did not learn institutional history quickly or well, nor did he understand faculty culture. He proved unable to deal with the structures and procedures that had slowly and sometimes painfully emerged in the system of faculty constitutionalism. The faculty's system of governance had proved quite effective, and they expected it to be used. The wheels of academic administration ground slowly under Pence, and false starts produced no results. Frequently, needed decisions were not made to support programmatic activity that was under way. All of this produced frustration.

While all understood that the provost's responsibilities were complicated, his administrative style and these problems were not serving the institution well in a period of remarkable advance. Jim Pence resigned in 2006.

He was replaced by professor of religion and specialist in American church history Patricia Killen. President Anderson said that after consultation with deans and faculty chairs to determine the best person to fill the role, when it ultimately came down to who heard the call to serve, "Patricia O'Connell Killen heard the call louder than others."[34] Killen, a graduate of Gonzaga University with a doctorate from Stanford, joined the faculty in 1989. She is the author or editor of several books including the important interpretive account *Religion and Public Life in the Pacific Northwest: The None Zone* (2004). She has served on most important faculty committees, as chair of the religion department, and as faculty chair.

There was greater flux in the School of Business. Donald Bell came as dean in 1998 and left four years later; longtime business professor Thad Barnowe filled in. After a complicated search James Clapper was appointed dean in 2004.

He was a professor of marketing at Belmont University (another ANAC school) in Nashville, Tennessee, who had served six years as dean of the School of Business at that institution. Prior to Belmont he had taught twenty years at Wake Forest University. It seemed like a good fit for PLU and the School of Business as it brought a greater international emphasis into its undergraduate curriculum and redesigned its MBA program. Shortly before the School moved into the Morken Center, Clapper left after one year to be president of Aladdin Temp-Rite Corporation, the North American subsidiary of a European manufacturer of food service equipment. Business faculty were shocked, but they quickly decided that forceful PLU graduate and one-time faculty member (1976-83) Andy Turner was what the school and institution needed.

Turner, with a 1981 Ph.D. degree from the Wharton School of the University of Pennsylvania, had joined the Frank Russell Company after his teaching stint, attracted by the leadership of George Russell, described by Turner as "the coolest guy I ever met."[35] He held various positions at the Russell Company, but left after twenty-one years because he wasn't having fun. "That is the only reason I ever left a job. It's all about the jazz. Life is way too short to do stuff you're not having a wonderful time with. There's too many things to do."[36] Very quickly, with two partners, he formed Northern Lights Ventures, a firm that finances the start-up of money manager teams. When offered the deanship, Turner consulted with his Northern Lights partners, did the arithmetic, decided he could manage an eighty-hour week, and accepted, "because I love the school."

His plans were dramatic. They included recruiting the best talent available (and raising the money to pay them), developing endowed chairs, requiring more publication, making classes more rigorous, and raising salaries to at least $150,000 a year.[37] The excitement in the School of Business was palpable. The plans seemed revolutionary to many both in and beyond the university. But on 26 April 2007, Turner reported to President Anderson that Northern Lights activity was developing much more rapidly than anticipated; pushed by his partners, he would have to resign the business deanship. The president was not pleased.

As President Anderson contemplated the situation it struck him that former Vice President for Finance and Operations Bill Frame, who had served the institution with great effectiveness in the 1990s and had retired a year earlier after nine creative years as president of Augsburg College, might serve the School of Business well in an interim capacity. Frame accepted Anderson's overture and began service on 1 September.

There was also instability in the development office. With the completion of "The Campaign for Pacific Lutheran University," David Aubrey left his leadership position in 2004. He was replaced by Executive Director of Development James Plourde in an interim capacity, In 2005 Rev. Stephen Cornils, a 1966 graduate of PLU and Choir of the West soloist, was named vice president for Development and University Relations. He had experience in management and stewardship through service at three churches in California, two in Minneapolis, and work as a communication consultant. He left after six months, however, discovering his calling remained the parish ministry.

In 2007 Steven Titus was appointed vice president. He had just concluded five years as president of Midland Lutheran College in Fremont, Nebraska. At Midland Titus also served as distinguished professor of leadership and change. He is a leadership coach, co-director of the Lutheran College and University Leadership Program, and adjunct executive coach and presenter for Leader Source, an international leadership and executive coaching firm.

Prior to joining Midland, Titus was executive assistant to the president at Gustavus Adolphus College in St. Peter, Minnesota (2000-2002), and a tenured professor of leadership studies and organizational behavior at Southwest Minnesota State University in Marshall, Minnesota (1997-2000). His credentials include a Ph.D. degree from the University of Virginia and a J.D. degree from Marquette University. He served as an attorney and commissioned officer in the U.S. Army Judge Advocate General's Corps from 1990 to 1995. Titus served as Minnesota's Civilian Aide to the Secretary of the Army from 1999 to 2002, and he was awarded the United States Army Outstanding Civilian Service Medal in 2002.

In fall 2007 PLU had one current and two former Lutheran college presidents in its administrative structure. The university community was eager to see how the institution would be served by a new provost and the talent and experience in its administrative sector.

In 2005 Paul Hoseth retired as director of athletics. He said it was never easy to decide when to leave, but he wanted to "help move us in the direction of improved funding and fund-raising for athletics and help lay the groundwork for new and expanded physical education, recreational and athletic facilities."[38] He was replaced by Laurie Turner, a Puyallup native and Washington State University graduate with twenty-five years of experience as a coach and administrator. She had served most recently at the University of California, San Diego, and before that at WSU, the University of Idaho, Eastern Oregon College, and the University of Toledo. She would serve as athletic director, but not also as dean of Physical Education, as had her predecessors David Olson and Hoseth. The AD position was too time-consuming, especially as details of the "Athletics, Recreation, and Physical Education Master Plan" of July 2006 emerged. That plan recommended that Memorial Gym, Names Fitness Center, and the swimming pool should be replaced with a new fitness and aquatics center, and then be demolished to make way for housing, parking, or academic buildings. The plan also suggested that Olson Auditorium should be renovated and new athletic fields should stretch into the golf course.[39] The new athletic director and the development staff would be busy.

Change also affected the School of Education. Lynn Beck resigned from the deanship in 2006, after seven years, to become education dean at the University of the Pacific. After a year of committee leadership in the school, John Lee was appointed dean. With a doctorate from the University of Illinois-Chicago, Lee had served in an administrative capacity at the University of Maryland-Baltimore and at Long Island University.

KPLU

One of PLU's greatest success stories from the 1980s onward was its National Public Radio station, KPLU. Launched in the mid-1960s as a ten-watt campus station, it advanced to 40,000 watts in 1972, and to 100,000 watts in 1980. Martin Neeb came from Los Angeles as general manager in 1981. He had been director of broadcasting for the Franciscan Communications Center which produced television and feature films. In 1983, under Neeb's leadership, the station changed to its distinctive jazz and news format; critics warned that the format wouldn't work, but it has been enormously successful.

The station has won numerous awards. Neeb boasts that KPLU is one of the best jazz stations in the world and one of the best NPR stations.[40] It produces 100 hours of music a week and 68 hours of news and special features, an unusual balance for an NPR station (the University of Washington's KUOW presents 11 hours of music and 157 hours of talk). As many as 500,000 listeners tune in each week via radio and the Internet, and more than 25,000 are paying subscribers[41]. With a budget of $4 million, the station is self-supporting, except for the infrastructure that PLU provides, allowing the station to operate without any daily overhead. Both parties have signed an editorial integrity statement to ensure the station's authority over what it broadcasts and how it portrays stories.

When Neeb retired as general manager in 2006, the university announced that funding for a new home for the station was almost complete, and that it would be named after him. This was made possible with a million-dollar gift from Larry Neeb, Martin's brother, a longtime regent and president of Creative Communications for the Parish, a St. Louis-based ecumenical publishing company. Designed to meet "silver" standards in the U.S. Green Building Council's LEED program, the new broadcast center will provide state-of-the-art facilities, environmentally stable storage for records and CDs, and badly needed improved and enlarged workspace. Construction began in January 2008. The building will serve the station well in the future, but Neeb will be missed. President Anderson declared that "you don't easily replace a star performer and manager like Marty. His vision and determination have literally transformed KPLU into a valuable community asset . . . that is a true point of pride for the university."[42]

New general manager, Paul Stankavich, was announced in January 2007. He came from Anchorage, Alaska, where he was president and general manager of Alaska Public Media. He has extensive experience in both public and commercial radio.

FACULTY APPOINTMENTS

In 2005, PLU's first fully endowed faculty chair was announced, the Benson Family Chair in Business and Economic History. The gift for the endowment came from 1963 graduate and regent Dale Benson and his wife, Jolita. After graduation Benson earned a Ph.D. in history at the University of Maine in 1970. He did research and taught at William and Mary and at Southwestern at Memphis. In 1971 he launched a second career in banking and finance, soon moved to Portland, Oregon, and ultimately founded Benson Associates, LLC. While teaching he discovered that business and economic history was badly taught, if at all, and decided that something needed to be done. The endowment was the Benson family's response.

The first holder of the chair was Professor E. Wayne Carp, an eighteen-year veteran of the history department with a doctorate in American history from the University of California at Berkeley. A demanding teacher, nationally known scholar, and author of four books, Carp is an expert on the history of adoption and secrecy and disclosure in the process of adoption.[43] In August 2007 it was announced that Carp had been awarded a Fulbright Distinguished Lecturer grant and would teach the following spring at Yonsei University in Seoul, Korea.[44]

An endowed professorship was announced in October 2007. The Kurt Mayer Professorship in Holocaust Studies honors the memory of family and friends murdered in the Holocaust. It was made possible by gifts from Kurt and Pam Mayer, Joe and Gloria Mayer, Natalie Mayer-Yeager, Nancy Powell, Carol Powell-Heller, and Harry Heller. Kurt Mayer, a Tacoma builder and the first Jewish member of the board of regents, escaped Germany in April 1940. Although concern about understanding and teaching about the Holocaust and genocide at PLU dates back to the 1950s, teaching and scholarship advanced significantly with Christopher Browning on the faculty after 1974. Further advances included the Raphael Lemkin undergraduate Holocaust and Genocide essay competition, established by regent Don Morken, and the annual Lemkin Lecture on the Holocaust and Genocide established in 2002. In November 2007 the first annual Powell and Heller Family Conference in Support of Holocaust Education was held. The two families are committed to teaching about the Holocaust throughout the Northwest to prevent its reoccurrence and foster understanding and respect.

The inaugural Mayer Professor was Robert P. Ericksen, a 1967 graduate of

PLU and a professor in the history department. A veteran teacher and much-published scholar, Ericksen has a Ph.D. degree from the London School of Economics and Political Science, and he is the author or editor of four books, including the definitive *Theologians Under Hitler*. His research has focused on the church and universities and university faculties in Nazi Germany.

Also in 2007, associate professor of Music Richard Nance was named the new director of choral activities and the Choir of the West. He is only the sixth person to hold that position since the choir was founded in 1927. Former director Kathryn Lehman was forced to resign because of ill health. Nance, a native of New Mexico, holds bachelor's and master's degrees from West Texas State University and a doctorate from Arizona State University. Both institutions have excellent choral music programs. He taught in several New Mexico and Texas high schools and then for seven years at Amarillo Junior College; he came to PLU in 1992. Nance intends to reduce the choir slightly, to about fifty members, and to create a pyramid of sound with power at the base and precision in all of the ensemble, but especially at the apex. He has also re-established the quartet system first introduced by director Maurice Skones (1964-83),[45] dividing the choir into quartets, not sections, with each quartet containing soprano, alto, tenor and bass voices. The effect blends voices within the entire choir, not just the section. He wants the choir to sing in a stylistically accurate fashion with historical perspective, within the limitations that the passage of time allows.[46] An active composer; Nance has composed twenty-nine choral works since 1983.

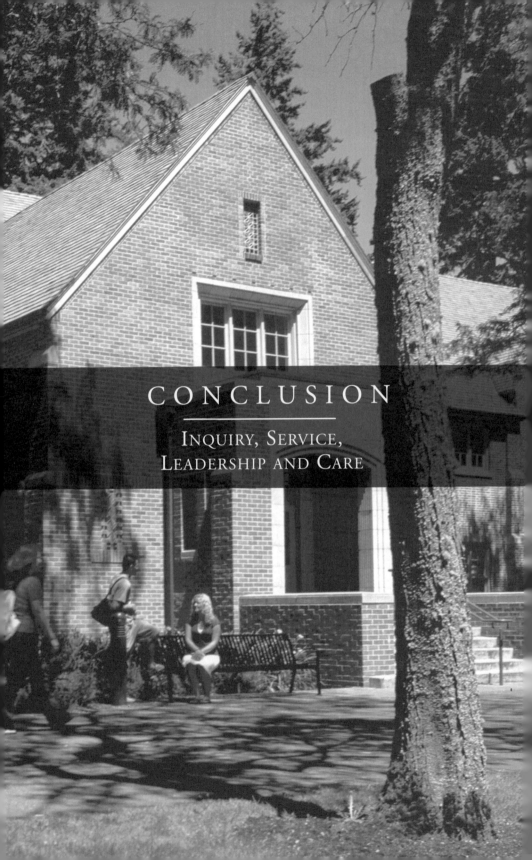

CONCLUSION

Inquiry, Service,
Leadership and Care

Conclusion

INQUIRY, SERVICE, LEADERSHIP AND CARE

IN THE YEARS STRETCHING from 1988 to August 2007, Pacific Lutheran University graduated 14,365 students with baccalaureate degrees: 2,705 in business, 1,921 in education, 1,373 in nursing, and the remainder distributed throughout the arts and sciences (1,658 received Bachelor of Science degrees). During the same period 2,877 master's degrees were conferred. Sixty-seven of the bachelor's degree recipients became Fulbright scholars, making PLU competitive with the better schools of its size and type around the country. (Since 1975, when Ann Mehlum was the first PLU student to receive a Fulbright, eighty-six graduates have received Fulbright awards or were alternative selections). Success was tied closely to the advice, encouragement, and prodding of longtime Fulbright advisor, German professor Rodney Swenson.

PLU also continued its success in getting its graduates into medical and dental schools. In the state of Washington PLU ranks second only to the University of Washington with the number of admissions to its medical school. The healing and service professions have been central to the institution's educational mission from the beginning.[1] The number of students going to graduate schools more generally has remained at a high level in the last two decades as well. Biology, chemistry, history, psychology and education are the leading units sending students to graduate school.[2]

Of all the graduates from recent decades, three reflect PLU's commitment to leadership, service, care, and a global focus in unique ways. Two are members of the United States Congress and the third served as the U.S. Ambassador to Namibia. It should be remembered that the first PLU graduate elected to Congress was the late Jack Metcalf. After serving for twenty-five years in the Washington state legislature he was elected to Congress in 1994 and served for three terms. Although not an alumnus, former faculty member Brian Baird has represented southwest Washington in Congress since 1998.

Lois Grimsrud Capps, a 1959 graduate of the School of Nursing, was elected to Congress in a March 1998 special election, replacing her husband, Walter, who had died of a heart attack the previous October. The decision to run was an agonizing one for her, but she wanted to continue the work Walter had begun. After a twenty-year career as a public school nurse, she won a narrow victory and continues to be re-elected by ever-increasing margins. In Congress she has focused on health care and education and has fought for the "vulnerable and powerless." She has attracted powerful allies. Former President Bill Clinton told a California audience that he had "never known a better human being than this woman, ever."[3] Capps thinks nursing school can provide "the perfect background" for service-minded students who might someday decide to run for public office.

1987 political science graduate Rick Larson won election in northwest Washington's second district in 2000. Just thirty-five, he had served three years as Snohomish County councilman. In a district with important military installations, he showed his political courage by voting against the invasion of Iraq, but he said he received little criticism for voting his conscience. He has been described as having a "natural instinct" for politics and a "down-to-earth" personality that serves him well. Former Washington State Transportation Chair Connie Niva said: "He's young, he's smart and he's gutsy. His district is very complicated, and he's a perfect match for it, because he's very bright, but he's also very tough."[4]

1976 graduate Joyce Barr chose a career in the foreign service at a time when there were relatively few women of color serving there. Her career has been distinguished by remarkable successes. She speaks Swedish (her first posting was to Sweden) and Russian and holds masters degrees from Harvard and The National Defense University. She has served in Kenya, Sudan, and Turkmenistan, and she worked on the AIDS epidemic in sub-Saharan Africa. She was ambassador to Namibia. In that fledgling democracy she keeps close tabs on PLU's connections with Namibia and on the young Namibians educated at PLU, who are playing such an important role in their country's government and educational system.[5]

SUCCESSES

The late 1980s and early 1990s were filled with enrollment and financial problems of a disturbing nature, but difficult decisions and determined leadership brought them under control. Both concerns require constant attention, but the institution is healthier demographically and financially in the twenty-first century than in the previous decade. Two successful fundraising campaigns have contributed to that health, and long-range plans have provided much clearer paths into the future. Badly needed buildings have been built: the Mary Baker Russell Music Center, the Morken Center, South Hall, and the Garfield Commons. Xavier Hall, the University Center, and several dormitories have been refurbished. President Loren Anderson's leadership was vital to these fundraising, planning, and building successes. Sustainability and environmental literacy became features of university life as well, expressed in a rich variety of ways, often by students.

The last two decades have seen remarkable advances in faculty scholarship, even though teaching remains the primary responsibility. The importance of vocation, always present in PLU life and teaching, has become more intentional with the "Wild Hope" project. PLU has also become a more globally focused university, as reflected in its curriculum, faculty accomplishments, study abroad participation, and campus activities. President Anderson told the Q Club in spring 2007 that because the challenges facing the global community were daunting, "this university has committed itself to seek to educate a new generation of global leaders who have the vision and the capacity and the will to build, in the words of our global education vision statement, a more 'just, healthy, sustainable and peace-filled world.'"[6]

STUDENT SATISFACTION INVENTORY

How have students reacted to their educations at PLU? Have they been satisfied with the education and activities provided? Have the values of the institution's educational philosophy had any impact on their life choices? To evaluate a wide variety of campus services the Noel-Levitz Student Satisfaction Inventory (SSI) has been administered seven times at PLU in ten years, beginning in 1996. The inventory's 116 items and twelve composite scales measure satisfaction with academic advising, campus climate, campus life, campus support services, concern for the individual, instructional effectiveness, recruitment and financial aid, registration effectiveness, safety and security, service excellence, student centeredness, and responsiveness to diverse populations. For 2006-07, the national normative data came from 284,992 students at four hundred four-year private institutions.

The 1996 composite scales found two items above the national mean, instructional effectiveness and student centeredness; five were at the national mean, and five registered below the national mean: recruitment and financial aid, registration effectiveness, academic advising, responsiveness to diverse populations, and safety and security.

As the university addressed problem areas with considerable vigor, each year's inventory detected improvement. In 2006 the best results over the ten year period were reached. Students rated PLU significantly above the national mean on ten of the scales, one scale at the national mean (responsiveness to diverse populations), and one below the national mean (safety and security). Major efforts to deal with these last two items have been made in the last decade. Vice President for Student Life Laura Majovski reported that "the results of the 2006-07 student satisfaction inventory indicate a very high level of satisfaction by PLU students on a wide variety of important scales."[7]

In 1998, on a more global scale, the Lutheran Educational Conference of North America (LECNA) hired an independent research firm to discover what Lutheran parents wanted from the college experience and what graduates of Lutheran institutions experienced. They compared those results with results from public flagship universities. The results and differences were striking. Lutheran educational institutions delivered on the claims and promises they made.

In career preparation and leadership, Lutheran institutions were more successful in helping develop effective speaking, effective writing, team participation, and leadership skills. Compared to the public universities, Lutheran institutions had a more teaching-oriented faculty (91 to 76 percent), more classes with fewer than twenty students, more personal interaction with professors (81 to 50 percent), and more interaction with students who share interests (83 to 70 percent). They offered more opportunities for internships and international study (44 to 22 percent), and much more opportunity to integrate values and ethics in classroom discussions (65 to 25 percent). The largest gaps were evident in the area of faith and spiritual development: more graduates of Lutheran institutions agreed, in the language of the inventory, that "college helped you integrate your faith into other aspects of your life" (60 to 10 percent), "you learned more about faith during your college years" (60 to 14 percent), and "there were faculty or staff after whom you modeled your spiritual life" (38 to 8 percent). The study concluded that 76 percent of Lutheran college graduates found their college experience "very effective at developing a sense of purpose in life—versus only fifty-seven percent of public university graduates."[8]

THE CHURCH

Despite these successes, PLU's relationship to the church has become more attenuated than any time in its history, especially at the national level. This is ironic, because the institution's identity has always been inextricably connected to the Lutheran church and its enthusiasm for education, fundamentally because the church recognized that education was needed to engage truth in all its multiform complexity.[9]

Frequently, the university was more concerned about the relationship than either the national church or local churches, but at its best the relationship flourished and benefits accrued for all. Evidence now suggests, however, that the relationship is stretching thin. What this means for the future is not clear. President Anderson discussed the situation in a 2004 speech at Carthage College.

> But change is all about us, and particularly since the formation of the ELCA, the church, preoccupied by other issues, challenged organizationally and financially, has been in retreat from this relationship . . . so while the church has backed away, the colleges, for the most part, have not . . . the church is seeking to reorganize in a manner that will diminish the voice of education and takes another major step toward the elimination of financial support.[10]

What can be done? Anderson told the audience at Carthage that PLU will shift from a program of church relations to an emphasis on congregational relations. Efforts will be made "to establish direct and supportive links with vibrant interested congregations . . . [and] all who care deeply about Lutheran higher education . . . As both synods and the national church withdraw, we look to these congregations as our natural Lutheran partners and foundations for the future."[11] How this works will have to be considered in the next history of PLU, but it marks a significantly new way of understanding the university's identity.

In these complicated and turbulent times, where flux often seems to be king, it is appropriate to give Martin Luther the last word. In times that were similarly complicated and turbulent, his enthusiasm for education remained constant.. About learning he is purported to have exclaimed a lapidary phrase that should be placed on the cornerstones of Lutheran educational institutions: "How dare you not know what can be known?" To public officials in Germany he wrote:

> Now the welfare of a city does not solely consist in accumulating vast treasures, building mighty walls and magnificent buildings, and producing a goodly supply of guns and armor. Indeed, where such things are plentiful and reckless fools get control of them, it is so much the worse and the city suffers great loss. A city's best and greatest welfare, safety, and strength consist rather in its having many able, learned, wise, honorable, and well-educated citizens.[12]

APPENDICES

Notes and Index

Draft Mission Statement, 1993

Now in its second century, embracing both its Lutheran heritage and the contemporary ecumenical environment, Pacific Lutheran University reaffirms its primary mission: to develop knowledgeable persons with an understanding of the human condition, an awareness of humane and spiritual values, and an ability to formulate and express ideas clearly and effectively. The university empowers its students for lives of thoughtful inquiry, service, leadership and care—for other persons, for the community, and for the earth.

To prepare students for these roles, Pacific Lutheran University fosters a climate of intellectual challenge distinguished by enthusiastic learning and committed teaching. The university is grounded in the liberal arts, which awaken the mind from ignorance and prejudice, expand capacities for reasoned conversation and creative innovation, and provide foundations for the highest standards of professional education and achievement. In a climate of free inquiry and expression, faculty and students alike seek to apply and advance knowledge and discern relationships among all branches of learning. Rigorous scholarship is enriched by active mentorship and collaboration.

Pacific Lutheran University is a diverse, caring community of students, faculty, and staff. As part of an increasingly interconnected and pluralistic society, the university welcomes different beliefs, backgrounds, and identities. Such diversity informs the search for truth, helps liberate the mind, and opens the heart to all humanity.

The university is dedicated to the education of body, mind, and spirit. It encourages integrated lives of physical activity and recreation, open discussion of all questions, empathetic encounters with difference, and worship and meditation. As a modern church-related university rooted in Martin Luther's affirmation of scripture, liberty, and conscience, Pacific Lutheran University supports the academic study of religion and helps students to develop informed perspectives on matters of faith and conviction. The university is committed to enlivening and sharpening constructive dialogue between an increasingly complex world and the community of the Church that confesses that life's ultimate meaning and hope are expressed in Jesus Christ.

University Income and Net Results, 1943-2007

Fiscal Year	Income	Gifts/Grants	Endowment
1943	$90,320	$39,017	$71,563
1944	149,274	106,476	68,626
1945	146,422	55,771	69,664
1946	171,314	49,042	72,182
1947	337,526	43,641	71,984
1948	537,854	44,584	75,608
1949	594,471	46,500	103,150
1950	647,308	52,195	115,193
1951	635,064	60,250	133,329
1952	634,564	84,140	139,299
1953	712,482	99,294	130,329
1954	787,101	113,228	141,195
1955	933,873	113,774	146,655
1956	1,161,829	125,860	269,710
1957	1,332,862	127,239	431,637
1958	1,535,014	142,783	453,882
1959	1,806,607	157,043	445,118
1960	1,913,980	163,328	459,826
1961	2,350,486	222,259	457,951
1962	2,445,469	254,118	448,337
1963	2,747,110	244,297	519,376
1964	2,947,481	294,668	549,606
1965	3,299,762	289,810	551,611
1966	3,727,181	338,024	560,134
1967	4,328,892	364,018	560,376
1968	5,378,996	512,221	710,059
1969	5,698,859	682,210	744,172
1970	6,189,137	625,325	698,073
1971	7,563,040	605,175	738,259
1972	7,942,110	661,467	1,053,325
1973	9,193,635	665,332	1,069,950
1974*	8,826,017	593,774	1,178,702
1975	10,519,634	665,046	1,178,562
1976	11,965,361	817,311	1,234,675
1977	13,422,817	1,387,503	1,295,937
1978	14,345,629	1,077,662	1,356,055
1979	16,724,700	1,176,001	1,472,856

University Income and Net Results, 1943-2007

Fiscal Year	Income	Gifts/Grants	Endowment
1980	18,539,273	1,060,041	1,623,750
1981	21,412,466	1,726,695	1,835,211
1982	25,152,864	1,644,091	2,048,173
1983	27,593,303	2,299,412	2,544,709
1984	30,083,490	1,841,605	2,920,533
1985	32,944,757	2,106,671	2,822,692
1986	35,186,794	2,831,317	3,534,031
1987	37,331,404	2,976,045	4,303,355
1988	41,309,860	3,123,224	5,146,365
1989	46,048,231	3,446,617	5,600,313
1990	47,180,545	3,269,591	6,781,002
1991	49,118,171	3,676,426	6,983,909
1992	50,445,279	3,924,833	8,150,415
1993	52,618,764	4,277,306	9,105,791
1994	54,172,985	4,074,059	14,623,294
1995	59,832,622	4,815,566	16,645,078
1996	53,141,670	8,154,677	20,680,639
1997	53,771,211	9,667,436	24,330,467
1998	55,620,459	10,918,270	30,736,017
1999	59,286,356	12,011,436	37,334,516
2000	64,825,733	14,583,150	43,618,993
2001	64,193,976	16,799,713	45,635,112
2002	66,946,993	16,731,166	45,079,532
2003	66,514,462	13,858,487	45,330,195
2004	73,581,533	18,824,001	51,480,542
2005	79,729,446	17,185,157	57,078,805
2006**	84,663,313	13,257,958	61,671,463
2007**	89,330,239	19,147,527	68,468,170

Fiscal Year changed to 1 June-31 May

**Unrestricted income less gift-funded capital projects*

Faculty Beginning or Ending Service in or After 1988

Name	Department	Dates of service
Adachi, Seiichi	Psychology	1967-1999
Adams, Harry	Physics	1958-1993
Adams-Kane, Jonathon	Economics	2007-2008
Ahn, Geun	Economics	2004-2005
Ahna, Barbara	Business	1980-81; 1987-2002
Aikin, Shirley	Nursing	1974-
Albers, James,	Business	1997-
Albrecht, James	English	1995-
Alexander, Angelia	Biology	1971-
Alleman, Judith	Nursing	2002-2003
Allen, Merrily	Nursing	1982-1988; 1991-2005
Anderson, Carl	Communication and Theatre	2003-2005
Anderson, Charles	Chemistry	1959-1991
Anderson, Dana	Psychology	1984-
Anderson, Loren	President	1992-
Andrews, Bradford	Anthropology	2005-
Ankrim, Ernest	Economics	1976-1992
Arai, Andrea	Anthropology	2004-2005
Arbaugh, George	Philosophy	1959-2002
Arnold, Denis	Philosophy	1995-2003
Arvey, Richard	Business	1992-1994
Atkinson, David	Political Science	1976-1997
Auman, Ann	Biology	2002-
Avila, John Paul	Art	2004-
Baird, Brian	Psychology	1986-1998
Baldwin, Marcia	Music	1995-2005
Bancroft, D. Stuart	Business	1967-1968; 1971-
Barndt, Stephen	Business	1978-2005
Barnowe, J. Thad	Business	1977-
Barot, Enrique	English	2005-
Barritt, Matthew	Education	1999-2003
Bartanen, Michael	Communication and Theatre	1979-
Basile, Laura	Nursing	2005-2006
Batker, Kenneth	Mathematics	1966-1999
Batten, Alicia	Religion	2000-
Baughman, Myra	Education	1970-2007
Beaulieu, John	Computer Science and Computer Engineering	1985-1995
Beck, Lynn	Education	1999-2005
Becvar, William	Communication and Theatre	1973-
Beegle, Amy	Music	2006-
Behrens Michael	Biology	2005-
Behrens, Michelle	Biology	2006-2008

Name	Department	Dates of service
Bekemeier, Luther	Office of Development	1976-1992
Bell, Donald	Business	1998-2003
Bell, Joanne	Nursing	2002-2007
Bell, Zelma	Communication and Theatre	2000-2001
Bell-Hanson, Jeffrey	Music	2002-
Benham, Steven	Geosciences	1982-
Benkhalti, Rachid	Mathematics	1987-
Benson, Carlton	History	1996-2005
Benton, Megan	English	1986-2005
Benton, Paul	English	1969-2007
Bergman, Charles	English	1977-
Berguson, Claudia	Languages and Literatures	2002, 2003-
Berman, Deborah	Computer Science and Computer Engineering	1995-1996
Bermingham, Jack	Social Sciences Division	1983-1996
Berniker, Eli	Business	1982-
Biblarz, Arturo	Sociology	1977-2005
Blaha, Kenneth	Computer Science and Computer Engineering	1989-
Bleecker, Cathy	Music	1989-1992
Blessinger, Todd	Mathematics	2000-2001
Bloomingdale, Daniel	Communication and Theatre	2004-2006
Bloomingdale, Wayne	Music	1999-
Blum, Dale	Biology	1998-1999
Borkowski, Wayne	Business	1997-1998
Box, Brian	Music	1998-2005
Bradley, Raydell	Music	1992-2003
Bradshaw, Mary	Nursing	1999-2004
Breazeale, Kathlyn	Religion	2001-
Brewer, Devon	Sociology	2000-2001
Bricker, J Arnold	Political Science	1971-
Brink, James	Computer Science and Computer Engineering	1970-
Broeckel, Jo Ann	Psychology	2000-2001
Brown, Elizabeth	Music	1999-
Brown, James	Music	2005-
Brown, Philip	Marriage and Family Therapy	2007-
Brown, R Michael	Psychology	1982-
Brown, Richard	Art	1986-1991
Brown, Roberta	Languages and Literatures	1979-
Brownell, Penelope	History	2005-2006
Browning, Christopher	History	1974-1999
Brue, Stanley	Economics	1971-
Brusco, Elizabeth	Anthropology	1988-
Bueler-Fong, Amy	Nursing	2003-2004
Buller, Thomas	Computer Science and Computer Engineering	1995-1996

Name	Department	Dates of service
Burke, Valerie	Chemistry	2003-2005
Burns, Pamela	Nursing	1994-1999
Butcher, Howard	Nursing	1993-1998
Byrnes, Ronald	Education/Instructional Development and Leadership	1998-
Cady, Jack	English	1986-1997
Cambier, Maureen	Nursing	1993-1994
Campbell, Thomas	English	1984-
Campos, Lee	Music	1992-
Capp, Grayson	Chemistry	2001-2002
Cardwell, Cheryl	Nursing	1994-1995
Carey, Andrew	Education	1988-1991
Carlson, John	Biology	1975-
Carlton, Brian	Social Work Program	1991-1992
Carlton, Susan	English	1991-
Carp, E. Wayne	History	1986-
Carpenter, Maryiva	Nursing	1974-1990
Carr, Judith	Special Academic Programs and Summer Studies	1979-2002
Carr, Mary Ann	Nursing	1997-
Cathcart, Adam	History	2007-
Ceynar, Michelle	Psychology	2001-
Chalmers, Ronald	Religion	2005-2006
Chase, Gary	Physical Education	1970-2006
Chastain, Patricia	Education	2000-2007
Chavez-Pringle, Maria	Political Science	2006-
Chhabra, Surjit	Business	2001-2005
Chilson, Clark	Religion	2005-2006
Christensen, Kirsten	Languages and Literatures	2004-
Christopherson, Kenneth	Religion	1958-1991
Chung, Weon	Computer Science and Computer Engineering	2000-2001
Churney, Marie	Education	1974-1998
Ciabattari, Teresa	Sociology	2007-
Cinnamon, John	Anthropology	1996-1999
Clapp, Jeffrey	Communication and Theatre	1995-
Clapper, James	Business	2004-2006
Clark, Andrew	Engineering	1987-1990
Clausen, Edwin	History	1983-1995
Clay, Keith	Physics	1995-1996
Cloyes, Kristin	Nursing	2004-2005
Cochrane, Brenda	Sociology	1989-1991
Collay, Michelle	Education	1998-2001
Cone, Dorothy	Nursing	1961-1991
Cooper, Keith	Philosophy	1984-
Corbett, Cynthia	Nursing	1995-1997
Corlett, J. Angelo	Philosophy	1992-1993

Name	Department	Dates of service
Cornwall, Glenn	Art	2006-2007
Corrigan, Corinne	Nursing	1992-1993
Cotten, Myriam	Chemistry	2002-
Cox, Dennis	Art	1972-
Crantz, Julie	Nursing	2002-2004
Crawford, Suzanne	Religion	2003-
Crayton, Michele	Biology	1977-
Croes, Dale	Anthropology	1983-1984
Crom, Matthew	Philosophy	2006-2007
Crum, Larry	Computer Science and Computer Engineering	1997-1999
Cruz, Maria	Anthropology	1992-1994
Culbertson, Jolene	Nursing	2002-2004
Dahl, David	Music	1969-2005
Damar, Halil	Economics	2004-
Darks, Gwendolyn	Nursing	2004-2007
Das, Kaustuv	Mathematics	1998-2000
Davidson, Emily	Languages and Literatures	2003-
Davidson, Jason	Communication and Theatre	1997-2000
Davis, Paul	Chemistry	2004-
Davison, Geoffrey	Physical Education	1991-1992
DeBower, Carrol	Education	1964-1968; 1970-1991
De Sherlia, Janet	Languages and Literatures	1982-1989
Desmond, Brian	Communication and Theatre	2005-
Detlor-Langan, Dorothy	Nursing	1989-1997
Di Stefano, Diana	History	2006-
Dietrich, Sydney	English	1990-1991
Dolan, Patricia	Biology	1994-2000; 2005-
Dollinger, Michael	Mathematics	1981-2003
Domby, Paul	Music	1991-1992
Dorner, Bryan	Mathematics	1980-
Dorner, Celine	Mathematics	1981-
Driessnack, Martha	Nursing	1999-2003
Dubois, Janet	Nursing	2003-
Duntley, Madeline	Religion	1990-1991
Dwyer-Shick, Susan	Political Science	1984-
Dybbro, Julie	Nursing	2000-2004
Easwaran, Shanmugalingam	Computer Science and Computer Engineering	2005-
Ebbinga, Spencer	Art	2006-
Edison, Larry	Computer Science and Computer Engineering	1982-2004
Edwards (Hefty), Luella Vig	Nursing	1973-2001
Egan, Maura	Nursing	1983-1992
Egbers, Gail	Library Information Services	1992-
Egge, Jacob	Biology	2007-

Name	Department	Dates of service
Ehrenhaus, Peter	Communication and Theatre	1998-
Ellard-Ivey, Mary	Biology	1997-
Ellis, Nancy	Nursing	1992-1995
Ericksen, Robert	History	1999-
Erickson, Susan	Music, 1994-	
Evans, Anthony	School of Physical Education/ Movement Studies and Wellness Educ.	1988-
Ewart, JoJean	Communication and Theatre	1990-1995
Eyler, Audrey	English	1981-
Fanslow, Julia	Nursing	1992-1993
Farid, Farid	Mathematics	2000-2001
Farmer, Donald	Political Science	1955-1991
Farner, Kathleen	Music	1978-
Farner, Richard	Music	1976-2007
Faustini, John	Geosciences	2000-2001
Faye, Louise Sand	Languages and Literatures	1969-1998
Feller, Amanda	Communication and Theatre	2000-
Ferguson, Chris	Information and Technology Services	2001-
Ferrer-Lightner, Maria	Languages and Literatures	2001-
Fesler, Diane	Nursing	2000-2001
Field, Hilary	Music	1984-2001
Finitsis, Antonios	Religion	2006-
Fink, Aileen	Nursing	1991-1994
Finnie, Bruce	Business	1989-
Finstuen, Andrew	Religion	2007-2008
Fischer, Marianne	Nursing	1995-1996
Fisher, Leslee	Physical Education	1992-1995
Fitzgerald, Shannon	Nursing	1992-1997
Fletcher, M Josephine	Education	1963-1991
Flynn, Bernadine	Nursing	2001-2002
Fofanov, Yuriy	Computer Science and Computer Engineering	1999-2000
Fofanova, Natalia	Computer Science and Computer Engineering	2000-2001
Foley, Duncan	Geosciences	1986-
Folsom, Michele	Computer Science and Computer Engineering	2000-
Ford, Teresa	Education	1993-1997
Forest, Adam	Economics	2002-2003
Fortune, Martine	Languages and Literatures	2005-2005
Franke, Melissa	Communication and Theatre	2006-
Frazey, Paul	Chemistry	1999-2000
Frenz, Annal	Religion	2006-2007
Frohnmayer, Mira	Music	1976-2005
Fryhle, Craig	Chemistry	1986-

Name	Department	Dates of service
Fuelling, Sarah	Psychology	1994-1996
Fukushima, Gary	Music	1996-2003
Gagnon, George	Education	1998-2000
Gard, Roger	Music	1974-2002
Gargano-Ray, Veeda	Anthropology	1985-1986; 1994-1995; 1999-00; 2001-2005
Garrigan, Dana	Biology	2000-2007
Garvey, Alan	Computer Science and Computer Engineering	1996-1997
Gaspar, Patricia	Nursing	1991-2007
Gee, Arthur	Biology	1968-2003
Gehring, Margaret	Physical Education	2006-2007
Gehrke, Ralph	Religion	1975-1990
Geller, Beatrice	Art	1984-
George, Pam	Nursing	1996-2005
Gerganov, Bogomil	Physics	2006-
Gerlach, Kent	Education/Instructional Development and Leadership	1980-
Gerstmann, Paula	Chemistry	1998-1999
Gibson, Linda	Business	1989-
Giddings, William	Chemistry	1962-1996
Gilbertson, William	Social Work Program	1968-1991
Gilchrist, Debra	Reference Librarian	1987-1991
Gilje, Fredricka	Nursing	2004-2005
Gilmore, Virginia	Library Information Services	1988-2004
Glasgow, Eilene	Education	1990-1997
Glover, Denise	Anthropology	2007-2007
Goedert, Kelly	Psychology	2001-2005
Gold, Lawrence	Art	1984-2006
Goodwin, Sheila	Nursing	1987-2000
Gough, Fern	Nursing	1971-1995
Govig, Stewart	Religion	1959-2001
Graham, Christina	Psychology	2006-
Grahe, Jon	Psychology	2005-
Green, December	Political Science	1992-1994
Greenwood, William	Physics	1981-
Gregory, Eileen	Biology	1999-2000
Gregson, Joanna	Sociology	1998-
Grieshaber, Kate	Music	1984-
Gross, Lora	Religion	1989-1992, 1999-2005
Grosvenor, Peter	Political Science	1996-
Guldin, Gregory	Anthropology	1979-
Gutmann, Robert	Computer Science and Computer Engineering	1989-1996
Hacker, Colleen	Physical Education/Movement Studies and Wellness Education	1979-
Haemig, Mary Jane	Religion	1994-1999

Name	Department	Dates of service
Hale, Connie	English	1989-1991
Hall, Dayna	Biology	2002-2003
Hallam, John	Art	1990-
Halvorson, Michael	History	2005-
Hames, Gina	History	1997-
Hansen, Constance	Nursing	1980-1991
Hansen, David	Biology	1974-2006
Hanson, Katherine	Languages and Literatures	1983-1993
Hanson, Marlis	Education	1971-1991
Hanson, Vernon	Social Work Program	1970-1999
Hansvick, Christine	Psychology	1979-
Haque, Kamaal	Languages and Literatures	2007-2008
Harmic, Edward	Music	1969-1991
Harmon, Susan	Business	2006-
Harney, Diane	Communication and Theatre	1992-
Harty, Jane	Music	1978-
Hassen, Judy	Education/Instructional Development and Leadership	2006-
Hasty, Jennifer	Anthropology	1999-2006
Haueisen, Donald	Computer Science and Computer Engineering	1980-1988; 1991-1996
Hauhart, Robert	Sociology	2005-2006
Hauser, George	Computer Science and Computer Engineering	1987-
Hayden, Richard	Education	1991-1994
Heath, Daniel	Mathematics	2002-
Hegstad, Larry	Business	1979-2007
Hendrickson, Kristi	Physics	1996-1996
Herman-Bertsch, Janet	Nursing	1984-1997
Herzog, John	Mathematics	1967-2003
Herzog, Margaret	Mathematics	1971-1996
Hesla-Kopta, Jean	Music	2000-
Heussman, John	Director of the Library	1976-1993
Hickey-Tiernan, Joseph	Religion	2007-
Hillis, Michael	Education/Instructional Development and Leadership	1997-
Hirsch, Anne	Nursing	1983-1998
Hoffman, David	Music	1975-
Hogan, Brendan	Philosophy	2005-
Holloway, James	Music	1990-2001
Holmgren, Janet	Languages and Literatures	2001-
Hoseth, Paul	Physical Education	1968-
Houston, Janeanne	Music	1989-
Howell, Nancy	Religion	1990-1998
Hua, Wei	Languages and Literatures	1988-1994
Huber, Curtis	Philosophy	1964-1991
Huelsbeck, David	Anthropology	1989-

Name	Department	Dates of service
Huestis, Laurence	Chemistry	1961-2004
Hughes, Patricia	Nursing	1992-1998
Hunnicutt, Lynn	Economics	2003-
Huston, Aaron	Nursing	2005-
Ihssen, Brenda	Religion	2005-
Immel, Don	Music	1997-1999
Inch, Edward	School of the Arts	1986-
Ingram, Paul	Religion	1975-
Jacks, Audrey	Instructional Development and Leadership	2007-2008
Jansen, Sharon	English	1980-
Jensen, Jo Ann	Biology	1967-1999
Jensen, Mark	Languages and Literatures	1989-
Jensen, Robert	Economics	1968-
Jett, Kathleen	Nursing	1995-2000
Jobst, Richard	Sociology	1967-2007
Johnson, Barry	Music	1989-
Johnson, Beverly	Nursing	1997-2000
Johnson, Gregory	English	1981-1991
Johnson, Gregory	Philosophy	1999-
Johnson, Gregory	Biology	2007-2008
Johnson, Neal	Economics	2004-
Johnson, Steven	Physical Education	2007-2008
Johnson, Wanda	Education	1989-1992
Jones, Richard	English	1969-
Joyner, David	Music	2000-
Kakar, Abdullah	Computer Science and Computer Engineering	1996-
Kalpin, Melissa	Information and Technology Services	1998-1991
Kang, Wenqing	History	2006-2007
Kaplan, Louise	Nursing	1996-2001
Kaufman, Rona	English	2002-
Kaurin, Pauline	Philosophy	1997-
Keeling, Bret	English	2004-2006
Kelleher, Ann	Political Science	1980-
Keller, JoDee	Social Work Program	1989-
Kelly, Frecia	Nursing	1990-1994
Kennedy, Michael	Biology	2000-2001
Kerk, David	Biology	1986-1992
Kerr, Rita	Nursing	2006-2006
Kerr, Stephani	Physical Education/Movement Studies and Wellness Education	2003-
Keyes, David	School of the Arts	1969-
Khan, Salah	Languages and Literatures	1998-2000
Kibbey, Richard	Business	1988-2002
Killen, Patricia	Office of the Provost	1989-

Name	Department	Dates of service
King, Gundar	Business	1960-1991
Kinzel, Dianne	Nursing	1992-1992
Kirkpatrick, Constance	Nursing	1980-1992
Kirkwood, Patricia	Library Information Services	1999-2004
Kittleson, Lars	School of the Arts	1956-2000
Klassen, Matthew	Mathematics	1995-1997
Klein, Laura	Anthropology	1979-
Klisch, Mary Lou	Nursing	1986-2002
Kluge, Mary Ann	Physical Education	1985-2002
Knapp, Calvin,	Music	1959-2000
Knapp, Sandra	Music	1971-
Knudsen, Jens	Biology	1957-1991
Knutson, David	Religion	1969-1991
Komjathy, Louis	Religion	2004-2005; 2006-
Kottal, Terri	Nursing	1987-
Kracht, Jerry	Music	1967-1968; 1969-2000
Kraig, Beth	History	1989-
Kratochvil, Dan	Business	1998-2000
Kurrus, Kent	Music	1999-2000
Lacabe, Maria	Languages and Literatures	1988-2004
Lacky, Donald	Mathematics	2000-2003; 2005-
LaFond, Rebecca	Biology	2004; 2006
Lamoreaux, C Douglas	Education	1994-2005
Land, Arthur	Communication and Theatre	2002-2003; 2004-
Lane Rasmus, Francesca	Library Technical Service	1998-
Lang, Renee	Physics	1994-1997
Lange, Annekathrin	Languages and Literatures	2005-2007
Lara, Maria	Psychology	1999-2001
Larson, Kristen	Physics	2000-2002
Lauer, Anthony	Business	1969-1992
LeBlanc, Patricia	Education	1997-1998
Lee, Chulho	Business	2006-
Lee, Chung-Shing	Busines	1998-
Lee, Dougla	History	1992-1996
Lee, John	Education and Movement Studies, School of/Instructional Development and Leadership	2007-
Lehmann, Kathryn	Music	2000-2007
Leitz, Paula	Education/Instructional Development and Leadership	1994-
LeJeune, Jerome	Psychology	1972-2006
Leon-Guerrero, Anna	Sociology	1993-
Lerum, Jerrold	Biology,	1973-
Levinsohn, Marilyn	Nursing	1992-2005
Levy, Matthew	English	2007-
Lewis, Jan	Education/Instructional Development and Leadership	1989-

Name	Department	Dates of service
Lindbo, John	Biology	1994-1996
Lisosky, Joanne	Communication and Theatre	1995-
Lizzi, Rhonda	Nursing	2006-
Long, David	English	2006-2006
Loughman, Henry	Communication and Theatre	2006-
Louie, Richard	Physics	1997-
Lovelace, Earl	English	1998-2005
Lowes, Brian	Geosciences	1968-
Lundeen, Lyman	Religion	1988-1989; 1990-1998
Lundgaard, Gene	Physical Education	1958-1991
Lyman, Zachary	Music	2006-
MacDonald, Diane	Business	1985-
MacGinitie, Laura	Computer Science and Computer Engineering	1993-1996
Madge, Sally	Education,	1993-1994
Mahoney, Barbara	Philosophy	1996-1997
Mahoney, Cynthia	Nursing	1981-1994
Main, John	Biology	1971-
Mallon, Ann Adele	Education	1987-1989
Maloney, George	Psychology	2004-2005
Maloney, Patsy	Nursing	1994-
Mandaville, Alison	English	2004-2005
Manfredi, Paul	Languages and Literatures	2001-
Manning, Chandra	History	2003-2005
Mansell, D. Moira	Nursing	1982-1994
Mar, Laureen	English	1992-1993
Marcus, Lisa	English	1995-
Mardis, Kristy	Chemistry	2000-2003
Marek, Jayne	English	1988-1995
Mariella, Anne	Nursing	2002-2003
Martin, Dennis	English	1976-
Martin, Dennis	Biology,	1975-2006
Martin, Gloria	English	1977-1991
Martinez-Carbajo, Paloma	Languages and Literatures	1999-
Martinson, Arthur	History	1966-2003
Mason, Andrea	English	2006-2007
Masson, Marilyn	Anthropology	1995-1996
Mathers, Marjorie	Education	1964-1966; 1968
Mathews, Heather	Art,	2007-
Matthaei, Charles	Business	1987-1991
Matthias, Dixie	Biology	1975-2002
Mayer, Shannon	Physics	1997-2000
McCallum, Larry	Information and Technology Services	2001-2002
McCann, Cherie,	Nursing	2003-2007
McCann III, Joseph	Business	1992-1998
McConnell, Karen	Physical Education/Movement	

Name	Department	Dates of service
	Studies and Wellness Education	1998-
McDade, Katherine	Sociology	1989-
McDonald, Susan	Library Information Services	1971-
McDowell, Teresa	Marriage and Family Therapy	2002-2003
McGee, Patricia	Education	1998-1999
McGill, Maureen	Physical Education/Movement Studies and Wellness Education and Communication and Theatre	1977-
McGinnis, Richard	Biology,	1972-
McGraw, Louette	Education	1995-1995
McKenna, Erin	Philosophy	1992-
McKenney, Rose	Environmental Studies Program/ Geosciences	2002-
McMullen, Roberta	Nursing	1996-1998
McNabb, David	Business	1979-2002; 2004-2007
Meister, Cecile	Biology	1996-1997
Menzel, Paul	Philosophy	1971-
Menzinger-Sjoblom, Lucia	Languages and Literatures	1997-1999
Meyer, Lawrence	Music	1969-1994
Meyer, N Christian	Mathematics	1970-
Mietzke, David	Communication and Theatre	2002-2005
Miller, Chip	Business	1991-2001
Miller, Joann	Nursing	1999-2002; 2003-2004
Miller, Marlen	Economics	1970-1996
Miller, Terry	Nursing	1998-
Milton, Andrew	Political Science	2000-2002
Minahan, Sue	Nursing	1992-1995
Miranda, Deborah	English	2001-2004
Miranda, Ines	Languages and Literatures	2000-2001
Mize, Emily	Nursing	2001-
Moe, Richard	Dean of the Arts and Graduate and Summer Studies	1965-1998
Mohtasham, Javid	Chemistry	1992-1992
Moon, Christine	Psychology	1990-
Moore, Bradford	School of Physical Education/ Movement Studies and Wellness Educ.	1980-
Moran, Mary	Social Work Program	2005-
Morford, Jennifer	Chemistry	2000-2000
Morgan, Paul	Communication and Theatre	1992-1993
Moritsugu, John	Psychology	1975-
Mosher, Darlean	Education	1984-1996
Mulder, Robert	Education	1987-
Murphy, Laurie	Computer Science and Computer Engineering	1997-
Mutchler, Jack	History	1999-2002
Myers, Gerald	Business	1982-

126   APPENDIX C

Name	Department	Dates of service
Myrbo, Gunnulf	Philosophy	1970-1994
Naasz, Brian	Chemistry	2005-
Nadine, Claudia	Languages and Literatures	2000-2002
Nance, Lewis	Music	1992-
Nelson, Eric	Languages and Literatures	1989-
Nelson, Gregory	Education	1992-1998
Nelson, Paul	Education/Instructional Development and Leadership	2005-
Nesset, Burton	Chemistry	1967-1998
Neudauer, Nancy	Mathematics	1998-2001
Neuffer, Julie	Religion	2002-2003
Newcomer Culp, Marilyn	Nursing	2001-2005
Ng'ang'a, Peter	Economics	2006-
Ngwa, Kenneth	Religion	2006-2008
Nissen, Ulrik	Religion	2005-2006
Nolan, Sheila	Communication and Theatre	1989-1992
Noll, Betty	Nursing	2005-2006
Nolph, Jesse	Psychology, 1968-1999	
Nordby, Jon	Philosophy	1997-2000
Nordholm, Eric	Languages and Literatures	1997-1997
Nordquist, Philip	History	1963-2005
Nornes, Sherman	Physics	1963-1991
Norton, Lisa	English	2004-2005
Nosaka, Akiko	Anthropology	2005-
Nugent, Rachel	Economics	1991-1999
Nussbaum, Rachel	History	2006-2007
Oakman, Douglas	Humanities Division	1988-
Oberholtzer, W Dwight	Sociology	1969-1995
O'Brien, Kevin	Religion	2006-
Oestreich, Joseph	English	2007-2008
Officer, Sara	Physical Education	1967-1998
Oka, Kayleen	Sociology	2004-2007
Okita, Lynn	Nursing	1998-2002
Olson, David	Physical Education	1969-2002
Olson, Franklin	Education	1971-1998
Olson, Kevin	Philosophy	1998-1999
Olson, Linda	Nursing	1967-2001
Olufs, Dick	Political Science	1982-
O'Neal, Thomas	Music	1988-1992
Owens, Helmi	Education	1983-2003
Page, Phyllis Lapine	Nursing	1997-1992
Palerm, Carmina	Languages and Literatures	2005-
Parker, Robert	Physics and Engineering	1987
Parker, Stephen	Physics	1999-2000
Parker, William	Communication and Theatre	1970-2005
Pass, Cleo	Nursing	1990-2004
Pence, James	Provost	2002-2006

Name	Department	Dates of service
Perkins, Jeannette	Nursing	1997-1998
Petersen, John	Religion	1967-2006
Peterson, Daniel	Religion	2005-
Peterson, Gary	Mathematics	1967-1998
Peterson, Gregory	Music	1990-1991
Peterson, Norris	Economics	1981-
Pham, Quoc Van Kien	Business	2002-
Phelps, Hannah	Philosophy	2007-
Philichi, Lis	Nursing	1990-1995
Pilgrim, Walter,	Religion	1971-1999
Pine, Judith	Anthropology	2006-2007
Poppe, Donna	Music	1998-1999; 2000-
Poulshock, Barbarba	Music	1976-1997
Powell, Edwin	Music	2005-
Pratt, Catherine,	Business	1983-
Predmore, James	Languages and Literatures	1977-
Ptak, Carol	Business	2005-
Radin, Patricia	Communication and Theatre	1999-2000
Rahn, Suzanne	English	1981-
Ramaglia, Judith	Business	1982-
Randolph, Timothy	Mathematics	1998-1999
Rasmussen, Janet	Humanities Division	1977-1991
Rasson, Judith	Anthropology	1984-1988
Raymond, Mary Anne	Business	1986-1989
Reid, Andrea	English	1997-1999
Reigstad, Paul	English	1947-1948; 1958-1990
Reiman, Mark	Economics	1988-
Reinhardt, Anita	Nursing	1992-1993
Reisberg, Leon	Education/Instructional Development and Leadership	1981-
Renaud, Michelle	Nursing	1994-2001; 2005-2007
Renfrow, Daniel	Sociology	2006-
Rhoades, Lois	Nursing	1980-1991
Richey, Edward	History	2007-
Rickabaugh, Karl	Education	1975-2000
Ridgeway, Kathleen	Nursing	2003-2004
Rieke, William O.	President	1975-1992
Riley, Martha	Communication and Theatre	1992-1995
Robbins, David	Music	1969-
Roberts, Steven	Nursing	2005-
Robinson, Marylou	Nursing	1993-2006
Robinson, Solveig	English	2001-
Rønning, Svend	Music	1999-
Rooney, Kathleen	English	2006-2007
Rosenfeld, Moshe	Computer Science and Computer Engineering	1986-2005
Rowe, Clifford	Communication and Theatre	1975-

Name	Department	Dates of service
Russell, Kathleen	Social Work Program	1999-
Sabeti, Roya	Physics	1992-1997
Sager, Kevin	Communication and Theatre	2003-2004
Savis, Jacqueline	Physical Education	1995-1997
Schafer, Eldon	Business	1974-1991
Schaffler, Ruth	Nursing	1992-
Schaffner, Mind	Nursing	2006-
Schenk, Suzan	Physical Education	1997-1998
Scherch, Jonathan	Social Work Program	1997-1998
Schiller, John	Sociology	1958-1991
Schlaefer, Ann	Nursing	1996-1996
Schultz, Carolyn	Nursing	1982-
Schultz, Jeffery	Chemistry	1998-2001
Schwidder, Ernst	Art	1967-1991
Scott, Damon	Mathematics	1986-1989
Scruggs, John	Business	1993-1995
Seal, David	English	1977-
Senn, Holly	Library Information Service	2002-
Sennett, James	Philosophy	1990-1992
Sepic, F Thomas	Business	1979-
Severtson, S. Erving	Psychology	1966-1983; 1986-2004
Shanton, Kyle	Education	1998-2003
Shore, Wendelyn	Psychology	1999-
Siegesmund, Amy	Biology	2007-
Simpson, Merlin	Business	1997-
Skendzic, Elizabeth	Biology	2005-2007
Skipper, Jaso	English	2005-
Sklar, Jessica	Mathematics	2001-
Smith, Bradley	Geoscience	1990-1991
Smith, Julie	Biology	2006-
Smith, Matthew	Biology	2001-
Smith-Garcia, Tara	Nursing	1989-1991
Snee, Rochelle	Languages and Literatures	1981-
Solheim, Bruce	History	1994-1995
Sosulski, Michael	Languages and Literatures	2000-2004
Sparks, Richard	Music	1983-2001
Spencer, Wallace	Political Science	1974-
Spicer, Christopher	School of the Arts	1978-2003
Spillman, Richard	Computer Science and Computer Engineering	1981-
St Clair, Priscilla	Economics	2001-
Staley, Jeffrey	Religion	1998-2000; 2004-2005
Starkovich, Steven	Physics	1996-
Starr, Marsha	Nursing	1995-1996
Stasinos, Michael	Art	2005-
Stewart, Sharon	Nursing	1993-1995; 2002; 2003-2007

Name	Department	Dates of service
Stiggelbout, Joan	Nursing	1973-1991
Stivers, Rober	Religion	1974-
Storfjell, Troy	Languages and Literatures	2005-
Storm, Cheryl	Marriage and Family Therapy	1985-2007
Stringer, L Allison	Physical Education/Movement Studies and Wellness Education	2006-
Strong, Carolyn	Nursing	1990-1991
Stuart, Jeffrey	Mathematics	2001-
Suarez, Alicia	Sociology	2006-
Sumner, Jeanie	Business	1989-1995
Swank, Duane	Chemistry	1970-
Swanson, David	Sociology	1987-1992
Swenson, Rodney	Languages and Literatures	1968-2000
Swett, Sara	Nursing	1999-
Sydnor, Darlean	Education	1984-1990
Szabo, Alexander	Sociology, Social Work Program	1994-2001
Talbert, Paul	Biology	1996-1997
Tang, Kwong-Tin	Physics	1967-
Tang, Ying	Computer Science and Computer Engineering	2001-2002
Tannehill, Deborah	Physical Education	1999-2006
Taube, Scott	Music	2003-2005
Taylor, Charles	Physics	1987-1991
Taylor, Marianne	Psychology	2005-
Taylor, Priscilla	Nursing	2001-2002
Taylor, Scott	Languages and Literature	2005-
Tegels, Paul	Music	2002-
Temple-Thurston, Barbara	English	1990-
Temple-Thurston, Peter	English	2000-2007
Templin, David	Physical Education	1998-2007
Terada, Kevin	Economics	2000-2004
Terpenning, Rae	Music	1987-2006
Teska, William	Biology	2000-
Thirumurthy, Vidya	Education/Instructional Development and Leadership	2005-
Thomson, Steven	Anthropology	2007-
Thrasher, Steven	Business	1980-
Thurman, Robert	Mathematics	1999-2000
Tjelta, Brenda	Chemistry	1996-1998
Tobiason, Fred	Chemistry	1966-1991; 2003-2005
Toczyski, Suzanne	Languages and Literatures	1996-1998
Tomko, Mary Kay	Nursing	2000-2004
Tomsic, Walter	Art	1970-
Tonn, Sheri	Chemistry	1979-
Torrens, Thomas	Art	1974-1989
Torvend, Samuel	Religion	1999-
Toven, Audun	Languages and Literatures	1967-2005

Name	Department	Dates of service
Toyokawa, Teru	Psychology	2002-
Travis, Karen	Economics	1998-
Trelstad, Marit	Religion	2001-
Tremaine, Ann	Music	1972-1991
Trudinger, Peter	Religion	2003-2004
Turner, Andrew	Business	1976-1983; 2006-2007
Upton, Joseph	Engineering	1988-1996
Vancil, Nancy	Music	1998-
Vancini, Margaret	Nursing	1991-2000
VanWyhe, Glenn	Business	1979-
Vaughn, Kevin	Anthropology	2001-2005
Vinje, David	Economics	1970-2005
Waldow, Dean	Chemistry	1992-
Walker, Diana	Music	2003-
Ward, David	Marriage and Family Therapy	2005-
Warner, Ding	Languages and Literatures	1997-2001
Waters, Gail	Business	1989-1992
Weber, Elizabeth Sue	Communication and Theatre	1995-1997
Webster, Paul	Languages and Literatures	1969-2006
Weiss, Janet	Education/Instructional Development and Leadership	2003-
Wells, Marjorie	Nursing	1998-1999
Wells, Robert	Communication and Theatre	2003-
Wells, Ward	Physical Education	2005-2007
Wentworth, Donald	Economics	1972-2002
West, Douglas	Communication and Theatre	1989-1992
Westering, Forrest	Physical Education	1972-2004
Wheeler, Christopher	Communication and Theatre	2006-2007
White, Joseph	Music	2001-2002
Whitman, Jill	Geosciences	1988-
Williams, Genevieve	Library Information Services	2005-
Williams, Gregory	Education/Instructional Development and Leadership	1985-
Williams, Tamara	Languages and Literatures	1994-
Williams-Ginsberg, Helen	Languages and Literatures	2001-2005
Wilson, Gary	Communication and Theatre	1975-1994
Woehrle, Margaret	Nursing	2000-2001
Wolf, Frederick	Business	2006-
Wolfer, Cynthia	Nursing	2001-2002; 2004-
Wolff, David	Computer Science and Computer Engineering	1999-
Woo, Hokwai	Computer Science and Computer Engineering	1988-1992
Wood, Nicole	Movement Studies and Wellness Education	2007-2008
Wood, Sylvia	Nursing	1993-
Woolworth, Stephen	Education/Instructional	

Name	Department	Dates of service
	Development and Leadership	2003-
Wrigley, John	Physics	1987-1994
Wu, Cynthia	Nursing	2005-
Wu, Dane	Mathematics	1994-
Xu, Jian	Economics	1999-2000
Yaden, Bridget	Languages and Literature	1996-
Yager, William	Business	1987-2007
Yagow, David	Associate Provost	1976-2003
Yakelis, Neal	Chemistry	2005-
Yerian, Suzanne	Education	1995-2003
Yetter, Cathleen	Education/Instructional Development and Leadership	1986-
Yie, Nancy,	Nursing	1997-2001
Yiu, Chang-li	Mathematics	1973-
York, Charles	Marriage and Family Therapy	1980-
Youtz, Gregory	Music	1984-
Yumibe, Yukie	Nursing	1980-1992
Zabriskie, Fern	Business	2001-
Zaichkin, Dana	Nursing	1997-
Zbaraschuk, Michael	Religion	2006-
Zhou, Yan	Computer Science and Computer Engineering	2002-2003
Zhu, Mei	Mathematics	1998-
Zulauf, Dwight	Business	1949-1953; 1959-1985; 1990-1998

Regents, 1896-2007

Alsaker, Daniel L.	1996-2007	Bryant, Neil R.	1988-1996
Anderson, Arthur I.	1958-1964	Burad, Becky	1997-2004
Anderson, H.E.	1925-1934	Burke, R.C.	1944-1947
Anderson, Herman E.	1962-1967	Bustad, John R.	1968-1974
Anderson, J.O.	1920-1926	Carlstrom, Theodore C.	1972-1977
Anderson, Jos. A.	1933-1935	Carr, Gwendolyn	1996-1998
Anderson, Mrs. Arnold F.	1950-1955	Chase, Goodwin	1970-1973
Anderson, N. Wm.	1933-1936	Christensen, M.A.	1900-1907;
Anderson, Olaf	1961-1964		1920-1922
Anderson, Thomas W.	1969-1996	Cornell, Donald E.	1964-1973
Armstrong, Jerold	1988-1996	Crary, Judson L.	1959-1960
Arntson, Neal L.	1996-2006	Daehlin, R.A.	1952-1956
Aus, Mrs. Alfred	1966-1974	Dahl, H.L.J	1938-1948
Baalson, H.E.	1912-1914	Dahl, Orville	1952-1953
Barbo, Linda	2006-	Dahlberg, E. John	1984-1987
Barton, E. Lee	1971-1974	Danielson, A.T.	1911-1914
Bauer, Richard L.	1996-2002	Davidson, O.K.	1936-1938,
Baughn, R. Gary	1980-1987		1952-1962
Belgum, Helen	1980-1988	Davis, George L. Jr.	1975-1987
Bemiller, Linda	1991-1992	Dederer, Michael	1964-1973
Bennett, Carl	1963-1972	Douglass, Ronald E.	1967-1973,
Benson, Dale	2002-		1986-1987
Berg, Gayle	2006-	Eckstrom, Earl E.	1953-1969
Berg, Gilbert	1965-1968	Edlund, Francis E.	1946-1952
Bevier, Deborah	1998-2001	Edwards, Cynthia Wilson,	1988-2006
Birkelo, R.C.	1935-1938	Eie, Leif	1980-1983
Bjerke, A.O.	1911-1913	Ellefson, T	1898-1900
Bjerke, Bruce	2005-	Ellman, Philip	1952-1958
Blaekkan L	1899-1901	Elmquist, O.A.	1941-1945
Bogstad, R.	1927-1933	Engstrand, Paul D.	1947-1950
Bolland, Marvin	1986-1987	Engstrom, Phillip	1962-1965
Bomgren, Charles	1979-1985	Engvall, R.F.	1939-1945
Bondo, Paul	1962-1973	Ericksen, Frank L.	1967-1973
Brevik, Karl	1962-1963	Erickson, Kenneth	1952-1957,
Brottem, J.O.	1898-1899		1966-1972,
Brueckner, Theodore C.	1964-1971		1977-1980
Brunner, Petra Onella	1988-1993	Evanson, Linda M.	1993-2002

Falde, Gaylerd	1951-1960	Halvorson, Mrs. Carl	1956-1962
Field, L.N.	1948-1951	Halvorson, Olaf	1938-1951
Fink, Alvin	1979-1988	Hamby, Darren	2007-
Fjellman, A.G.	1963-1967	Hansen, Chester	1968-1974
Foege, William	1997-2006	Hanson, Dennis	1986-1987
Ford, M.H.	1927-1930	Harstad, Bjug	1896-1901
Ford, Morris	1942-1951	Hartman, Connye	1996-1997
Forde, M.H.	1928-1936	Hartmann, M.K.	1938-1941
Foss, H.L.	1942-1963	Hartvigson, Ken Jr.	1996-2007
Foss, L.C.	1903-1904;	Hatlen, Roe	1997-2006;
	1906-1911		2007-
Foss, Michael	1988-1991	Hauge, Lawrence	1972-1978
Fuhr, M.J.K	1942-1953	Haukeli, G.R.	1928-1935
Fynboe, Carl T.	1967-1976	Heimdahl, O.E.	1920-1931
Gallaway, George H.	1964-1968	Hellman, W.H.	1946-1949,
Gates, James	1981-1987		1954-1961
Getzendaner, David C.	1964-1970	Henriksen, George	1922-1931
Gomulkiewicz, Robert	2002-	Herbert, Jesse E.	1970-1973
Gonyea, Douglas	1971-1974	Hildahl, Richard	2002-
Goodnow, Roberta	2001-	Hilderbrandt, Emery	1974-1977
Gornitzka, O.	1920-1922	Hofstad, Robert	2001-
Grahn, Clarence A.	1957-1960	Hoglund, Paul	1973-1989
Grant, R. Gene	1972-1978	Hokenstad, M.T.	1934-1942
Grant, Roland L.	1978-1981	Holen, O.	1920-1923
Greenwood, David	2002-	Holmquist, Ruth	1984-1987
Grewenow, George	1966-1969	Hong, Nils	1901-1915
Grewenow, Ronald D.	1988-1995	Howard, Robert	1988-1997
Grimsrud, J.M.	1960-1961	Hubbard, Howard	1979-1986
Gronsberg, O	1896-1897	Husby, Glen	1968-1974
Groschupf, J.M.	1934-1936	Hushagen, James	1992-1999;
Gudmunsen, O.S.	1940-1944		2004-
Gulbrandsen, J.Olaf	1927-1933	Irby, Galven	1969-1988
Gunderson, P.	1909-1911	Jacobson, Kathleen	1998-2007
Haavik, O.L.	1927-1935	Jeffries, Mrs. Ruth	1972-1978
Hadland, Robert	1974-1980	Jennings, Frank	1984-1997
Hafer, Anne	1996-2005	Jensen, J.L.	1896-1897
Hageness, N.N.	1939-1952	Jenson, J.M.	1930-1934
Hageness, Olai	1950-1955,	Johnson, Darcy	2003-
	1960-1963	Johnson, Elmer M.	1934-1941
Hager, Connye	1988-1997	Johnson, Katherine	1998-2007
Halvorson, Halvor	1965-1968	Johnson, Theodore L.	1990-1996

Kelley, Estelle	2005-		2000-
Kettner, A.R.M.	1935-1942,	Long, Michelle Y.	2001-
	1945-1948	Lorentzsen, Norman	1965-1971
Keys, Michael	2005-	Losnes, Chr.	1898-1907
Kirkebo, B.L.	1914-1915;	Ludwig, L	1930-1945
	1920-1926	Lund, Carl A.V.	1946-1955
Klein, Richard	1973-1988	Lund, Clarence	1958-1960
Klockstad, E.	1912-1914	Luvaas, P.J.	1932-1939
Kluth, Lee	1985-1988	Maier, Donald	1997-2003
Knorr, E.C.	1934-1946	Martin, J.Orville	1948-1950
Knudson, Mark	1996-2001	Martinson, Ronald D.	1982-1988
Knudson, Melvin	1969-1986	Mason, F.C.	1934-1940
Knudson, Mons	1902-1910	Mayer, Kurtis K.	1996-2005
Knutson, Lowell	1963-1969	McKean, Michael	1980-1981
Knutzen, Beverly	2004-2007	McKinney, Wallace G.	1985-1995
Knutzen, Chris	1947-1958	Milbrath, John	1979-1983
Knutzen, Einer	1956-1969	Mills, Fred	1952-1953
Knutzen, George	1940-1947	Moe, Jordon	1981-1984
Knutzen, Victor F.	1980-1983	Moilien, Margaret	1963-1970
Knutzen, Victor	1969-1972	Molter, F.J.	1949-1958
Koester, Jerrold	1974-1977	Morgan, Harry	1980-1988
Koosmann, Konrad	1949-1955	Morken, Donald	1988-1998;
Korsmo, Lisa	2007-		2002-
Kraabel, Alf M.	1934-1943	Morken, E.A.	1948-1966
Krippaehne, William W.	1996-2004	Mueller, Richard E.	1989-1995
Kvinsland, Jon	2006-	Muenscher, Frederick	1979-1981
Kyllo, Eldon	1955-1959	Mykland, A.A.	1935-1950
Lagerquist, George	1978-1987	Myron, H.	1920-1923
Larsen, N.A.	1911-1913	Natwick, Phillip	1969-1975
Larsen, P.T.	1911-1912;	Neeb, Larry W.	1996-2003;
	1921-1926		2005-
Larsen, Tobias	1896-1903	Neils, Richard	1974-1980
Larson, Christine	1988-1991	Nelson, A.W.	1952-1957
Larson, Ingebret	1898-1902	Nelson, Harold E.	1962-1968
Larson, Kenneth C.	1960-1962	Nelson, John	1969-1976
Larson, Ludvig	1941-1944	Nelson, Suzanne	1977-1980
Larson, Roger C.	1972-1981	Nesse, Kathryn	1952-1968
Lekness, A.L.	1925-1928	Nesselquist, Kim	2005-
Lerch, Ronald	1976-1979	Nestande, C.E.	1951-1952
Lindblom, L. Myron	1958-1961	Newcomb, Robert	1980-1986
Long, Anne	1989-1998,	Nieman, Gus	1960-1962

Norgaard, C.H.	1946-1954	Rouse, Richard	1991-1997
Norgore, Martin	1947-1954	Russell, Jane	1988-1997
Norswing, Knute B.	1928-1935	Rygg, Sterling	1974-1980
Oakley, John	1988-1997	Sachse, Kathleen McCallum	2005-
Odell, C.S.	1935-1939	Saetra, T.C.	1896-1897;
Ofstedal, R.A.	1941-1945		1908-1911
Olson, Jon	1988-1997	Sahlin, Gerry Anne	1996-2003
Olson, Knut	2005-	Sandgren, Carl H.	1944-1946
Omland, Richard	2002-2008	Sather, John	1959-1962
Ordal, O.J.	1913-1915;	Saverud, Wayne P.	1988-1996
	1920-1922	Schimke, Gerald E.	1968-1977
Orvik, Florence	1975-1978	Schlitt, Donna	2006-
Ottoson, Lisa	2005-	Schmidt, O.A.	1942-1952
Oyen, Arndt	1940-1942	Schnaible, Dorothy	1974-1987
Paulson, Casper F.	1977-1986	Schwarz, M. Roy	1971-1980
Paulson, Eric	1962-1971	Scott, Howard O.	1966-1975
Peters, David	2007-	Severson, Gary	1988-1993;
Peterson, Arthur M.	1988-1995		1996-2007
Peterson, Clayton B.	1975-1984	Shjerven, Rebecca Lucky	1996-2007
Peterson, Conrad	1968-1971	Siefkes, S.C.	1949-1957;
Pflueger, Jesse	1970-1979		1960--1965
Phillips, Karen	2000-	Sigloh, Frank	1972-1975
Pihl, Martin	1976-1982;	Sloan, Richard	1988-1989
	1997-2006	Sorenson, S.L.	1953-1955
Probstfield, Jeff	1981-1990	Stauffer, Jim	1997-2006
Quello, Robert	1973-1979	Steen, David	1980-1995
Quigg, Carol Sheffels	2004-	Stevens, Otto	1991-2000
Ramseth, Mark	1999-2002	Stime, E.V.	1962-1964
Ramstad, Anders	1922-1923	Stone, Alfred	1970-1976
Ramstad, William	1983-1994,	Strain, F. Warren	1973-1979
	1996-1999	Strand, Arne	1941-1955
Randall, Alvin	1963-1966	Stratton, Robert	1962-1966
Randall, William S.	1985-1988	Stringer, Susan	1997-2006
Randolph, Paul V.	1938-1942	Stub, H.A.	1910-1911;
Rasmussen, L.	1925-1926;		1914-1915
	1930-1943	Sture, Vernon	1986-1987
Rippey, Jeffrey	2001-	Swanson, C.R.	1933-1940
Roe, K.N.	1946-1948	Swenson, S.L.	1954-1960
Rogge, Barry	1988-1996	Taylor, Donald	1973-1976
Rolander, Doris	1978-1984	Tellefson, Eileen	2005-
Ross, B. D.	1922-1929	Tenwick, John	1940-1942

Thorpe, H.J.	1935-1938
Tjernagel, H.M.	1904-1906
Tollefson, E. Duane	1969-1972,
	1984-1986
Tommervik, Martin	1954-1958
Turner, Andrew	2004-2006
Ufer, Karl	1967-1970
Ulleland, Christy	1975-1995
Urness, Nyer	1965-1967
Vaswig, John L.	1996-2005
Victorson, Harry V.	1949-1950
Vigeland, Karen	1986-1991
Vigness, Paul	1947-1954
Virak, Roy	1980-1988
Vraalsen, Tom Eric	2006-
Wade, George A.	1973-1985
Waldum, H. Peder	1964-1968
Wang, Peter	2003-2006
Wehmann, George	1988-1995
Wells, Martin	2001-
Wells, Robert	1961-1962
Westerberg, Paul	1945-1947
White, Elmer J.	1963-1969
Wick, Donald M.	1988-1996
Widsteen, Harold	1954-1962
Wigdahl, A.O.	1956-1960
Wigen, Jan	1989-1992
Wigstrom, Dean II	1996-2005
Wilson, Donald	1991-2000
Wold, David	1972-1987;
	1998-2001
Woldseth, Edroy	1959-1962
Xavier, J.U.	1914-1915
Yee, Andrew	2005-
Ylvisaker, J.N.	1932-1945

—N O T E S—

CHAPTER ONE
THE CENTENNIAL CELEBRATION AND AFTERWARD

1. Committee members included Thom Sepic, Professor of Business, chair; Lucille Giroux, Executive Associate to the President; Joe Coffman, Director of Media Relations; John Heussman, Director of the Library; Edgar Larson, Director of Planned Giving; Philip Nordquist, Professor of History; Janet Rasmussen, Associate Professor of Languages; and Walt Shaw, Director of Alumni Relations. Added later were Betty Helseth, class of 1966, and Regent David Steen.
2. "100 Alumni Receive Centennial Recognition," *Scene* (December 1990).
3. For the honorees see *Scene*, ibid., and the "Centennial Alumni Recognition" booklet, which provides pictures and brief biographical sketches.
4. Daniel Callahan was director of the Hastings Center, Terrel Hill was senior health advisor to the United Nations Children's Fund, Margretta Styles was professor of nursing at the University of California at San Francisco, Thomas Weller was retired from the School of Public Health at Harvard, and Salim Yusuf was a leader in the development of large-scale clinical drug trials at the National Institute of Public Health.
5. *Scene* (March 1991).
6. 3 June 1990.
7. Aug. R. Suelflow, Director, Concordia Historical Institute, to Philip A. Nordquist, 19 June 1991.
8. 4 November 1988 and 18 November 1988
9. *Mooring Mast*, 7 April 1989.
10. "The State of the University, 1989" (8 September 1989), Rieke File, PLU Archives.
11. *Mooring Mast*, 11 May 1990.
12. Ibid., 28 September 1990.
13. "The State of the University, 1990" (7 September 1990), Rieke File, PLU Archives.
14. President William Rieke to Dr. Norris Peterson and Dr. Donald Wentworth, 18 September 1990, Peterson Files.
15. Norris Peterson and Don Wentworth to President William Rieke, 21 September 1990, ibid.
16. Norris Peterson to President William O. Rieke, 28 September 1990, ibid.
17. *Mooring Mast*, 8 March 1991.
18. Ibid., 12 April 1991.
19. Ibid., 13 September 1991.
20. Norris Peterson and Donald Wentworth to Loren Anderson, President, and David Hawsey, Dean of Admissions, 8 March 1993, Peterson Files.
21. For information on Hunthausen and the honorary degree controversy see the material in Board of Regents Correspondence, 1959-1991, Box 22, PLU Archives.
22. David C. Wold to Jeffrey L. Smith, 22 May 1991. Regents File, Box 22, PLU Archives.
23. *Mooring Mast*, 3 May 1991.
24. Ibid., 9 December 1988.
25. Ibid., 7 April 1989.
26. *Scene* (March, 1990).
27. *Mooring Mast*, 17 November 1989.
28. Ibid.

29. President William Rieke to Faculty, Students, Staff (15 January 1991), Rieke File, PLU Archives.

30. 30 November 1990.

31. William Rieke, "Weaving Us Together — Our Christian Vocation," Devotion for NW and SW Synods, ELCA, Region I (16 June 1990), Rieke Memoranda and Speeches, 1988-92, PLU Archives.

32. Philip A. Nordquist, *Educating for Service* (Tacoma, WA, 1990), 165-67.

33. Ibid., 169.

34. See the FRoG file in the Browning Papers, PLU Archives.

35. *Mooring Mast*, 3 April 1992.

36. Ibid., 11 May 1990.

37. President William Rieke to Faculty, Staff, Students (5 November 1990), Rieke Memoranda and Speeches, 1988-92, PLU Archives.

38. The commission members were: Faculty, Colleen Hacker, Paul Menzel, Philip Nordquist, Leon Reisberg, Sheri Tonn, Dwight Zulauf; Staff, Margaret Childress, Mary Olson; Administration, Rob Patterson; Student, Beth Goode.

39. President Rieke to the Pacific Lutheran University Community (20 March 1991), Rieke Memoranda and Speeches, PLU Archives.

40. *Mooring Mast*, 19 April 1991.

41. Ibid., 26 April 1991

42. "The State of the University, 1991" (6 September 1991), Rieke Memoranda and Speeches, PLU Archives.

43. See *Educating for Service*, Chap. 10.

44. *Mooring Mast*, 8 May 1992.

45. Ibid.

46. Board of Regents Minutes (April 26-27, 1992), PLU Archives.

CHAPTER TWO
A NEW PRESIDENT, OLD PROBLEMS, INTERESTING BEGINNINGS

1. Report to the Presidential Search Committee of Pacific Lutheran University from the Academic Search Consultation Service, 5 August 1991. All information about the presidential search is from my files.

2. For this biographical information see Frank Jennings's memorandum to "The Pacific Lutheran University," 11 November 1991.

3. The *Mast*, 25 November 1991.

4. Frank Jennings, "Presidential Search–Summary Update" (29 November 1991), Nordquist files.

5. The *News Tribune*, 16 December 1991. See also Scene (December 1991). Kenneth Tolo stayed on at the University of Texas at Austin, and in 1992 Ryan Amacher was appointed president of the University of Texas at Arlington. In 1995 he resigned, saying "he was tired of having his reputation attacked and his property vandalized." The resignation "shocked" faculty members, who had scheduled a no-confidence vote about his leadership. Critics charged that too much money was spent on athletics and entertainment and he gave the provost too much control over departmental matters (*Chronicle of Higher Education*, 17 March 1995).

6. The *Mast*, 7 February 1992.

7. *Educating for Service*, 176.

8. *Scene* (October 1992).
9. Ibid.
10. I was present at the luncheon, as was Christopher Browning.
11. Frank Jennings to the presidential search committee, 9 September 1992.
12. The *Mast*, 11 September 1992.
13. *Scene* (December 1992).
14. Minutes of the President's Strategic Advisory Commission meeting, 11 April 1991.
15. Philip Nordquist to Keith Cooper, Lyman Lundeen, and Douglas Oakman, 3 June 1991.
16. Minutes of the President's Strategic Advisory Commission, 12 September 1991.
1. The *Mast*, 20 September 1991.
18. Ibid., 1 May 1992.
19. Philip Nordquist, "Presentation to Regents," 12 October 1992, Nordquist files. See also Educating for Service, 223-25.
20. Loren Anderson to the PLU community, 14 October 1992, Nordquist files.
21. Ad hoc committee on the mission statement to PLU Faculty, 5 February 1993, attached to faculty meeting agenda.
22. Minutes, meeting of the faculty assembly, 12 February 1993.
23. The *Mast*, 19 February 1993.
24. Ibid., 26 February 1993.
25. Report to the PLU Board of Regents, 1 February 1993, PLU Board of Regents file, President's Office.
26. PLU Board of Regents file, 22 February 1993, ibid.
27. Anderson letter, Nordquist files.
28. Minutes, meeting of the PLU Board of Regents, 3 May 1993, Regents files, President's Office.
29. *Scene* (June 1993), 11.
30. "Regents' correspondence," 25 November 1992, Regents files, President's Office.
31. Board of regents executive committee telephone conference call, 6 January 1993, ibid.
32. The *Mast*, 5 February 1993.
33. Bill Frame to Philip Nordquist, 16 August 2006.
34. Ibid.
35. Ibid.
36. Loren Anderson to the PLU community, 7 June 1993. Presidential memos, PLU Archives.
37. Faculty Handbook, 1995, 134-37.
38. Loren Anderson to all faculty, 29 March 1995. Presidential memos, PLU Archives.
39. Board of Regents agenda and minutes, 26-27 January 1996, Regents' files, President's Office.
40. Linda N. Hanson, "Restructuring Academic Programs: Faculty Leadership in Effective Organizational Change." Ed.D. diss. abstract, Seattle University, 1999.
41. Presentation by Linda N. Hanson, Pacific Lutheran University, 27 May 1999.
42. The *Mast*, 25 September 1992.
43. For this information see the scrapbook in the music department office: "MBR Construction and Opening and Music Department Photos."
44. Ibid.
45. Loren Anderson to PLU faculty and staff, 25 October 1996. PLU Archives.

Chapter Three
Governance and Planning

1.   The *Mast*, 2 December 1994.
2.   *Scene* (October 1992). Professor Porokhov lectured at PLU in October 1991.
3.   Ibid.
4.   The *Mast*, 8 September 1995.
5.   Committee members were Shirley Aiken, John Herzog, Rochelle Snee, and Wally Spencer, chair.
6.   Report to the faculty from the ad hoc committee on faculty governance, 5 February 1993. Nordquist files.
7.   Ibid.
8.   The first eight faculty chairs were: Christopher Browning, 1993-95; Patricia Killen, 1995-96; Philip Nordquist, 1996-98; Dennis M. Martin, 1998-2000; Norris Peterson, 2000-02; Michele Crayton, 2002-04; Charles Bergman, 2004-06; Erin McKenna, 2006-08.
9.   See PLU 2000: Embracing the 21st Century (Tacoma, Wash., 1995), and Philip A. Nordquist, PLU 2000: In Retrospect (typescript, n.d.). An attached document, PLU 2000: The Results, compiled by staff, summarized progress toward the axioms' and initiatives' goals. The PLU 2000 bibliography lists the papers written for the eight study commissions.
10. The *Mast*, 3 December 1993.
11. Ibid., 3 February 1995.
12. Ibid., 24 September 1993.
13. Ibid., 8 October 1993.
14. Ibid., 18 November 1994 and 2 December 1994.
15. Ibid., 8 March 1996.
16. Ibid., 29 March 1996.
17. Ibid., 12 April 1996. The ten were Scott Kessler, Scott Westering, Susan Westering, Frosty Westering, Nick Dawson, Brian Brennt, Mike Benson, Craig McCord, Mark Woldseth, Leslie Woldseth.
18. The letter was signed by Lisa Marcus, Arturo Biblarz, John Moritsugo, Laura Klein, Tamara Williams, and Michael Bartanen.
19. The *Mast*, 12 April 1996.
20. *Scene* (Summer 1996).
21. Ibid., Spring 1997.
22. Ibid.
23. Ibid.

Chapter Four
A New Millennium

1.   For faculty publications from a slightly earlier period see *Faculty Scholarly and Professional Accomplishments*, June 1, 1989 - May 31, 1990, and *The Faculty Scholar at Pacific Lutheran University*, vol. 1, August 1990. Nordquist file.
2.   See Philip A Nordquist, "A Brief History of the Pacific Lutheran History Department" in *A Lutheran Vocation: Philip A. Nordquist and the Study of History at Pacific Lutheran University*, ed. Robert D. Ericksen and Michael J. Halvorson (Tacoma, WA.: PLU Press, 2005).

3.   The *Mast*, 6 March 1998.
4.   Ibid., 30 October and 6 November 1998.
5.   Ibid, 16 March 2001 and 7 December 2001.
6.   Ibid., 5 February 1999.
7.   ANAC mission statement, approved October 1995.
8.   The *Mast*, 12 February 1999.
9.   *Scene* (Fall 1999).
10.   *Sports Illustrated*, 14 August 1990, 104.
11.   Ibid., 105.
12.   *Scene* (Spring 2001).
13.   Ibid (Winter 2003).
14.   4 December 2003 and 19 October 2003.
15.   The *Mast*, 17 September 1999.
16.   Ibid., 9 November 1999.
17.   Ibid., 3 December 1999.
18.   Ibid., 18 February 2000.
19.   Ibid.
20.   Ibid., 3 March 2000.
21.   6 November 2000, Nordquist files.
22.   5 November 2000, Nordquist files.
23.   "Report of the Commission on Campus Climate," 13 March 2001. The members were Rick Rouse, Sarah Allen, Richard Louis, Kathleen Farrell, Aaron Bell, Jennifer Wrye, Erik Samuelson, Michelle Pleny, Norris Peterson, and Diane Harney.
24.   *The Daily Flyer*, 8 May 2000.
25.   "Report on Selected Campus Ministries," prepared by students, summer 2000, 7.
26.   The *Mast*, 15 September 2000.
27.   Ibid., 29 September 2000.
28.   Ibid., 20 October 2000.
29.   Ibid., 23 February 2001.
30.   Ibid., 2 March 2001.
31.   Ibid.
32.   The five were Capital University, Gonzaga University, Seattle University, the University of Portland, and the University of Dayton.
33.   "Should PLU Accept the Offer to Become a Host Institution for ROTC? A Collection of Information and Opinion Pieces to Assist Faculty in Considering Motions at the April 20, 2001 Faculty Meeting."
34.   Minutes of the meeting of the faculty assembly, 20 April 2001.
35.   The *Mast*, 11 May 2001.
36.   *Prism* (Division of Humanities, Spring 2002), 5.
37.   Ibid.
38.   Jaroslav Pelikan, *The Vindication of Tradition* (New York and London, 1984), 65.
39.   *Prism*, 5.
40.   *Scene* (Fall 2002), 35-37.

Chapter Five
Internationalizing the Institution

1.   Pacific Lutheran College *Bulletin* 16, no. 4 (January, February, March 1937), 1.
2.   Philip A. Nordquist, "A Brief History of the PLU History Department," in *A Lutheran Vocation*, 15.
3.   *Educating for Service*, 164.
4.   Ibid., 215.
5.   Ibid.
6.   Ibid., 216.
7.   Ann Kelleher, interview with author, 19 July, 2006.
8.   *Scene* (Spring 2002), 5.
9.   Ibid.
10.   Ibid. (Summer 2003), 15.
11.   Ibid.
12.   Ibid. (Spring 2005), 7.
13.   Ibid. (Spring 2006), 14. Sobania came to PLU in fall 2005 after twenty-four years at Hope College, his *alma mater*, where he was director of international studies and professor of history, with specialization in African history, especially Ethiopia and Kenya. His Ph.D. is from the University of London.
14.   "Distinctive Hallmarks of International Education," Pacific Lutheran University (type-script, n.d., n.p.), Nordquist files.
15.   *News Tribune*, 22 April 2007, E 1.
16.   Ibid., E 4.
17.   The *Mast*, 14 February 2003.
18.   Ibid.
19.   *Scene* (Fall 2004), 16.
20.   *PLU 2010: The Next Level of Distinction* (January 2003), foreword.
21.   Ibid., 4.
22.   Ibid., 29.
23.   *Scene* (Summer 2006), 18.
24.   Ibid.
25.   Ibid., 16.
26.   Ibid., 17.
27.   *News Tribune*, 6 June 2006.
28.   *Campus Voice*, Pacific Lutheran University, 5 January 2007.
29.   *Viewbook 2005-06* (Pacific Lutheran University, 2005), 29.
30.   *Scene* (Winter 2004), 13.
31.   Ibid. (Winter 2006), 18.
32.   Ibid.
33.   The *Mast*, 13 September 2002.
34.   *Scene* (Fall 2006).
35.   The *News Tribune*, 4 February, 2007, Section D.
36.   Ibid., D 6.
37.   Ibid.
38.   *Scene* (Summer 2005).
39.   *Athletics, Recreation, and Physical Education Master Plan* (Pacific Lutheran University, July 2006), 43.

40. *Scene* (Winter 2002).

41. The *News Tribune*, Sound Life (10 May 2004).

42. *Campus Voice*, 9 September 2006.

43. *A Lutheran Vocation*, 14.

44. *Campus Voice*, 9 August 2007.

45. Paul Benson, "A Brief History of the Choir of the West: 75 Years of Service and Choral Excellence" (typescript, n.d., n.p.) 2.

46. Richard Nance, interview with author, 28 September 2007.

CONCLUSION
INQUIRY, SERVICE, LEADERSHIP AND CARE

1.   *Educating for Service*, 107, 116.

2.   Ibid., 230.

3.   *Scene* (Fall 2005), 10. For Lois Capps's battle against the tobacco industry's efforts to sell a new product to young women, Camel No. 9, see Anna Quindlen, "Killing the Consumer," *Newsweek* (1 October 2007), 92.

4.   *Scene* (Fall 2005) 11.

5.   Ibid. (Winter 2004).

6.   Ibid. (Fall 2007), 38.

7.   *Pacific Lutheran University Student Satisfaction Inventory, 2006-07* (typescript), 5.

8.   *The Lutheran College Advantage: Values-based Communities of Learning* (LECNA, Sioux Falls, South Dakota, 1998).

9.   Joseph Sittler, "Church Colleges and the Truth," in Connie Gegenbach, ed., *Faith, Learning and the Church College: Addresses by Joseph Sittler* (Northfield, Minn., 1989), 27.

10. Loren Anderson, "Private University, Public Witness: Life in the 'None Zone,'" The Vocation of a Lutheran College Conference, Carthage College, 1 August, 2004, 14-15. Nordquist files.

11. Ibid., 15-16.

12. Martin Luther, "To the Councilmen of All Cities in Germany That They Establish and Maintain Schools," Walther I. Brandt, ed., *Luther's Works*, 45 (Philadelphia, 1962).

INDEX